HOW ARE WE GOVERNED?

CONTEMPORARY CANADA: ISSUES AND INSIGHTS

Editor: John Saywell

HOW ARE WE GOVERNED?

John Ricker
John Saywell

CLARKE, IRWIN & COMPANY LIMITED
TORONTO, VANCOUVER

© 1971 by Clarke, Irwin & Company Limited

First published in Contemporary Canada Issues and Insights edition 1971

ISBN   0 7720 0510 9

7 8 9 10   JD   80 79 78 77

Printed in Canada

CONTENTS

ACKNOWLEDGMENTS

The authors and publisher wish to thank Historical Services and Consultants Limited, Toronto, Ontario, for their help in researching the cartoons for this book.

The authors and publisher also wish to thank the following organizations which made available the cartoons appearing on the pages listed.

Robert Chambers—*The Halifax Chronicle-Herald* / 60, 75, 133; John Collins in *The Montreal Gazette* / 142; Miss Julie Dale and Peter Kuch of *The Winnipeg Free Press* for the Arch Dale and Kuch cartoons / 108 (Dale); 112 (top), 129 (Kuch); 164 (both Dale); Macpherson in the *Toronto Daily Star*, Reprinted with permission of *Toronto Daily Star* / 19, 28, 31, 34, 36, 43, 62, 70, 78, 113, 118, 155; *The Montreal Star* / 57 (Racy); 82, 123 (McNally); Len Norris and *The Vancouver Sun* / 127; Roy Peterson in *Maclean's* Magazine, 1968 / 45; Public Archives of Canada / 39, 42, 101, 106; Reprinted with permission of *The Globe and Mail*, Toronto / 125; Rusins in *The Ottawa Citizen*, Reprinted with permission of *The Ottawa Citizen* / 5, 74, 119; *The Toronto Telegram* / 80 (Grassiuk), 112 (bottom, Andy Donato).

PREFACE

Canada in 1971 is a far different country from the Canada of the late 1950's when an earlier version of *How Are We Governed?* was first planned. The old certainties have long since disappeared; and the solutions to new problems are by no means clear. A nation that once complained that politics were dull has lived through crises that have captured headlines around the world. Above all, the revolution in Quebec has forced a radical rethinking of the nature of our state and society, and the fanatics of the F.L.Q. have destroyed whatever complacency we may have felt about the stability of Canadian society and even the survival of the state.

How Are We Governed? is designed to provide the background to and some insight into the working of government and politics in Canada. There are many books describing Canadian government. Most of them could be entitled *How We Are Governed,* for they trace with loving attention to form and detail the institutions of Canadian government and the smooth working of the Canadian governmental system. Yet institutions do not work the way they are supposed to, and their operation is seldom smooth. This brief volume attempts to look at how government does work, at the political forces behind the governmental facade, at the defects as well as the virtues. It may raise more questions than it answers.

How Are We Governed? attempts to be up-to-date. Between the time the book went to press and the writing of this Preface the apparent agreement on the constitution reached at Victoria in mid-June 1971 has been rejected by Quebec. By the time the book is published, Quebec may have changed its mind again or the new government of Saskatchewan—elected a few days ago—may have adopted a different position than the old.

John Ricker
John Saywell

Toronto, July 1971

1 GOVERNMENT DEFINED

If on Monday ten people were shipwrecked on a desert island, by Saturday they would probably have established some form of government. For government is simply the organization of men for common action. Even primitive societies have machinery for maintaining law and order and getting things done.

Life without government would be difficult to imagine. The seventeenth-century English philosopher, Thomas Hobbes, compared it to a war of "every man against every man." In such a situation, he wrote, ". . . there is no place for industry, because the fruit thereof is uncertain, and consequently no culture of the earth, no navigation nor the use of commodities that may be imported by sea, no commodious building, no instruments of moving and removing such things as require much force; no knowledge of the face of the earth; no account of time, no arts, no letters, no societies; and, which is worst of all, continual fear and danger of violent death, and the life of man solitary, poor, nasty, brutish and short." It is one of man's greatest triumphs that he has solved the problem of the constant war of "every man against every man" by means of government.

What is Government?

Among civilized peoples government does not exist merely to provide law and order, but that is its essential function, since without order nothing else is possible. Government provides the means by which men can accomplish, as a group, work that the individual alone cannot possibly do. At one time the function of government was restricted to such primary tasks as maintaining law and order, collecting taxes and conducting foreign affairs and

3

defence. Today, there are few aspects of our private or public affairs that are not regulated or affected in some way by government. Whenever we switch on a light, turn a tap, post a letter, eat a piece of meat, take a pill, drive along the highway or attend a school or university, we are making use of services supplied or regulated by some level of government. The most important single fact about modern governments of any kind in any country is that they are Big Governments and likely to become even bigger. In highly complex societies government is one of the most complex, varied and pervasive of all human institutions.

In forming their government, our shipwrecked islanders would have many choices. They might agree to accept the rule of the most intelligent, or the handsomest or the shortest, and make him a king or a chief. They could have chosen a leader by picking straws, or by a show of hands or by a secret vote. The strongest might have imposed his will on the group by force and become a dictator. If they could not agree among themselves on a common policy, the ten castaways might have organized themselves into two or more groups, in which case there would be two or more governments, each with a different solution to the common problems. The possibilities are endless, and each choice would lead to a different kind of government.

Once equipped with a government, by the end of a week the castaways would probably have devised a simple set of rules and regulations or a constitution which defined the rights the individual enjoyed and the responsibilities he owed to the group or the public. By the end of a year this simple system would have become much more complex and there would undoubtedly be some arrangement for enforcing the rules.

Regardless of what kind of government the islanders chose, it would almost inevitably consist of three parts: legislative, executive and judicial. This is true not only of the government of a country, but for most clubs as well. A full meeting of the club members usually passes certain broad proposals, which can be called legislation. These

"A federation requires a very delicate balance" – Prime Minister Trudeau

So too does the establishment of any form of government, for both man and his world are unbelievably complex.

meetings, however, are held infrequently. To carry on the work of the club on a day-to-day basis, the members elect an executive—a President, Secretary, Treasurer and other officials. Finally, many clubs have sets of rules and regulations concerning the behaviour and activities of the members and have judicial bodies which act as a form of court to judge those charged with disobeying the club laws.

The Government of Canada

What kind of government has Canada? The answers to this question will be found in the remaining chapters of this book. Here we shall consider, in a general way only, some of the many replies that Canadians might make if the question were put to them. Some might answer a democratic government, others a Liberal government, others monarchical government, parliamentary government, responsible government, cabinet government, federal government and so on. Each of these answers is in its own way correct, for each refers to a particular feature of the Canadian government.

Those who reply that Canada has a democratic government are really talking about the way we choose our rulers.
The word democratic comes from the Greek *demokratia*,
which is a combination of two Greek words, *demos*, people, and *kratos*, power. In other words, the people have
power, or the people rule. Since it is obviously impossible
today for all of the people in any country to govern, democracy in modern states means basically a system in
which people freely choose their governments. In a democracy like Canada, this is done by having the voters elect
representatives to govern them. These representatives are
our servants, not our masters.

When people say that we have a Conservative or Liberal
government, they refer neither to the form nor the working
of government but to the political party which controls the
government. Political parties provide the fuel and energy to
drive our political system. Without them, government as
we know it in Canada would simply not be possible.

Those people who answer that Canada is a monarchy
are quite correct, for in theory the Queen, represented in
Canada by the Governor-General, is the head of the government and the source of all authority. In practice, however, as we shall see later, the role of the monarch or the
Governor-General in government is very small. Thus, people who say that Canada's government is monarchical are
thinking about the form of Canadian government rather
than the way it actually works. If a foreigner knew only
that Canada was a monarchy, he would have a hopelessly
misleading idea of the nature of our government.

The answer parliamentary government comes much
closer. By parliamentary government we mean a government carried on by Parliament, which in Canada consists
of the Queen, represented by the Governor-General, an
appointed Senate and an elected House of Commons. In
England, Parliament, which began as a very minor part of
government and was dominated by the king, gradually
came to share power with him. After the Revolution of
1688, when the English people drove out one king and

invited another to the throne, Parliament became the real ruler of England. The king's ministers, the men who did the actual work of governing the country, then gradually came to be responsible not to the king but to the elected House of Commons.

In Canada we have adopted the basic principles of the British parliamentary system. The ministers, or cabinet ministers, as they are called, must have seats in the House of Commons or the Senate, and they must retain the support of a majority of Members in the House of Commons to stay in office. Canadians who use the term *responsible government* to describe our system are referring to this *responsibility of the Cabinet or executive branch to the House of Commons or legislative branch*. Because executive power and a good deal of legislative power rest in the Cabinet, many Canadians refer to our system as cabinet government.

Those who reply that Canada has a federal government are referring to the fact that government in Canada operates on two different levels: the provincial and the national. The national government and the provincial governments each have definite powers and responsibilities which are outlined in a written document, the British North America Act of 1867. In other words, legislative authority or the power to make laws is divided between the central government at Ottawa and the ten provincial governments. Because of this division of power, Canada is a federation, or has a federal system of government.

Each of these aspects of Canadian government and politics must be discussed more thoroughly. Only when each has been understood will the complex structure and working of Canadian government become intelligible.

2 THE WORKING OF DEMOCRACY

Canada has representative government, a system whereby the people govern themselves through representatives of their choosing. These representatives make up the House of Commons. To elect Members of the House of Commons, the country is divided into two hundred and sixty-two geographical areas known as constituencies or ridings. (Two constituencies, Queen's County in Prince Edward Island and Halifax in Nova Scotia, elect two Members, making two hundred and sixty-four Members in the House of Commons in all.) In each constituency the political parties select a person to contest the election. On election day the candidate receiving the largest number of votes is declared elected and takes his seat in the House of Commons. The party which wins the most constituencies will, under normal circumstances, form the government. The leader of the victorious party will become the Prime Minister. The voter thus votes not only for a candidate, but for a political party and a Prime Minister as well. On the surface the election of a government appears to be a very simple matter and easily understood. Beneath the surface, however, it is much more complex, and raises many problems and debatable issues.

Who Can Vote?

Today, in national elections every man and woman has the franchise, or the right to vote, if he is eighteen or over, is a Canadian citizen or a British subject who was qualified to vote in the 1968 election and has resided in Canada for twelve months before the election. Since 1970 British subjects, like all other immigrants, must become Canadian citizens before they can vote. Such widespread suffrage is

8

known as universal suffrage. Members of the armed forces may vote regardless of age, on the principle that a man old enough to fight for his country is old enough to vote. Disqualified are judges, those civil servants who supervise the elections, criminals, lunatics and people found guilty of dishonest practices in previous elections.

The same qualifications and restrictions generally exist in the provinces, though there are minor variations in the franchise regulations. In Saskatchewan, Quebec, Manitoba and Prince Edward Island eighteen-years-olds are allowed to vote in municipal and provincial elections, and in Alberta, British Columbia, Nova Scotia and Newfoundland nineteen-year-olds have the same right. As this book goes to press, the Ontario and the New Brunswick legislatures are considering bills that would lower the voting age from twenty-one to eighteen.

The wide franchise enjoyed today was not won overnight or without a struggle. The great Reform Bills passed in 1832, 1867 and 1884 in Great Britain mark major and dramatic episodes in the popular struggle to obtain the vote. In Canada, the process was much less dramatic; there were no threats of revolution as there were in England in 1832; there was no powerful aristocracy to protect its privileged position as the ruling class, for pioneer life did not encourage the development of an aristocracy. When Upper and Lower Canada were given representative institutions by the Constitutional Act of 1791, the right to vote was restricted to men who owned a small piece of property, who paid twenty dollars rent a year or who earned over three hundred dollars a year. Under these qualifications, most adult males could vote. In 1888 Manitoba and Ontario adopted a manhood suffrage which entitled all men to vote when they reached the age of twenty-one, whether they owned property or not, and the federal government followed suit in 1920. The province of Quebec did not adopt manhood suffrage in provincial elections until 1936, however.

In their battle for the right to vote, the women of Can-

DISTRIBUTION OF SEATS

Ontario	88
Quebec	74
Nova Scotia	11
New Brunswick	10
Manitoba	13
Saskatchewan	13
Alberta	19
British Columbia	23
Newfoundland	7
Prince Edward Island	4
Yukon, N.W.T.	2
Total	264

In terms of population Prince Edward Island should have only two seats in the House of Commons; but in 1867 it was agreed that no province should have fewer seats in the Commons than in the appointed Senate. Prince Edward Island was given four Senators and so has four Members of Parliament. This was done at the request of the small provinces which felt that in time they would be swamped by the larger provinces.

ada did not interrupt debates in Parliament, tie themselves to lamp-posts, throw acid in mail boxes or jump under racehorses, as did English women. But if their methods were less spectacular, Canadian women were no less determined. One of the most determined was Mrs. Nellie Mc-Clung, one of the leaders of the Votes for Women Movement in Manitoba. In 1914, twenty years after women first asked for the vote, Mrs. McClung presented a petition to Premier Roblin, who gently reprimanded her and refused to let her speak to the Cabinet:

> Even if they listened to you, which I doubt, you would upset them and I don't want that to happen. They are

good fellows; they do what they are told. Every government has to have a head and I am the head of this
one and I don't want any dissentions and arguments.
You can't come here and make trouble for my boys
just when I have them trotting easy and eating out
of my hand. Now you forget all this nonsense about
women voting. You're a fine, smart young woman, I
can see that. And take it from me, nice women don't
want to vote.

Later Mrs. McClung used her showmanship to mock
Roblin at a public meeting. Imagining a situation in which
a delegation of men had come to her—the Premier—with a
petition demanding the vote, Mrs. McClung addressed
them in the manner in which Roblin had answered the
women:

We wish to compliment this delegation on their
splendid and gentlemanly appearance. If without exercising the vote, such splendid specimens of manhood
can be produced, such a system of affairs should not
be interfered with. Any system of civilization that can
produce such splendid specimens is good enough for me
—and if it's good enough for me it's good enough for
anyone. Another trouble is that if men start to vote
they will vote too much.

While Roblin continued to denounce the Votes for
Women Movement as one supported only "by men who
wear long hair and women who wear short hair," the agita-
tion proved successful. The Liberals accepted the principle
of female suffrage and, after their victory in 1915, gave
women the vote in 1916. Saskatchewan and Alberta followed
in the same year, while British Columbia and Ontario did
so in 1917, Nova Scotia in 1918, New Brunswick in 1919
and Prince Edward Island in 1922. The federal government granted women the franchise in 1918 (although close
female relatives of servicemen had been allowed to vote in
the wartime election of 1917, since the government calcu-
lated that they would support conscription). It was 1940
before women were allowed to vote in Quebec provincial
elections. The right of women to hold public office in Canada was generally recognized when they were granted the

franchise. Some women have made outstanding contributions to public life in municipal politics. Some have sat in the provincial legislatures and the Parliament of Canada, and it appears now to be accepted that, if possible, one should be a cabinet minister in the federal government. We have yet to have a woman as Prime Minister of Canada or a provincial Premier. Ceylon led the Commonwealth in choosing a woman as Prime Minister in 1960 and India followed a few years later with the selection of Indira Gandhi.

Quantity or Quality?

Many people assume that the quality of government is directly related to the number of people who vote. It is true that without a wide franchise the few would govern the many, and this is undesirable. But is it wise to push the question of numbers too far; to go as far, for example, as those who cry at election-time, "It doesn't matter for whom you vote, or why you vote, as long as you get out and vote"? Of course it matters! Fifty votes cast by people who know the issues, who have considered the problems facing the country and who know how the parties propose to solve them are worth more than one hundred votes cast in ignorance. Is there not a danger of confusing democracy with numbers, and quantity with quality? The ideal would be to have one hundred per cent of the voters cast their ballots intelligently. Today a third—two-thirds and more in municipal elections—of those who have the right to vote do not care enough about their government to walk a few blocks to the polling booths and mark their ballots. Moreover, it is unlikely that even half of those entitled to vote could pass a simple test on Canadian government and public affairs. Concerned with such ignorance, some observers argue that there should be some kind of political literacy test, as there is for new citizens. But the proposal raises so many problems that it has never gained widespread support, and the votes of the informed and the ignorant are given equal consideration in our elections.

One Man, One Vote?

Some of the opponents of political literacy tests contend that they are not democratic. They point out that democracy rests on the principle that in choosing our rulers the vote of every individual should count for the same: one man equals one vote. But no sooner is this principle stated than we raise another problem, for in Canada the simple truth is that every vote does not have equal weight. There is a gap between the democratic ideal of equality and actual political practice. The two hundred and sixty-four federal constituencies in Canada are divided among the ten provinces according to their population, and this division is reviewed every ten years after the census has been taken. Each province, therefore, is represented fairly, having a number of seats roughly corresponding to its share of the total population of Canada.

One would expect that each constituency would include roughly the same number of voters. Only then would every vote have equal weight. But such is not the case. Before the federal constituencies were reformed in 1966, three constituencies had fewer than 12,000 people, while several had over 200,000. This same imbalance, which favoured the rural areas at the expense of the rapidly growing cities, could be found in the distribution of seats for the provincial legislatures.

In recent years, however, there has been remarkable progress in improving the representative system. In 1963 the Liberal government in Ottawa passed a redistribution bill to cut out the worst anomalies. For the first time in Canadian history an independent commission was created to carry out a thorough redistribution of seats. (Previously the government had rearranged the constituencies and had often been accused—usually justly—of gerrymandering, that is, of arranging the boundaries of the ridings so as to enhance their own prospects and hurt those of the opposition.) The commissioners were instructed not to vary more than 25 per cent in creating ridings of equal population. When the commission reported in 1965, few ridings in all of Canada remained the same. In Quebec, for example, surgery was performed in every riding except Verdun, and in Ontario only two ridings emerged unchanged. In Quebec and Ontario most of the new constituencies would have between 60,000 and 70,000 people, whereas formerly Isles de Madelaine had 12,000 and Montreal Mercier, 233,000. Naturally, there were howls of protest from Members of Parliament, as well as the occasional charge of gerry-mandering. But in 1965-66 the foundations were laid for the most drastic redistribution in Canadian history and for a much more representative democratic system.

Nevertheless, this massive redistribution still did not create ridings of equal population. Many rural ridings fell below the average, while many urban ridings were above and some even exceeded the 25 per cent margin. The cities, on the whole, remained under-represented. Montreal, Toronto, Vancouver and Winnipeg still sent fewer Members to Ottawa than their population warranted. In the federal election of 1968, 63,000 people voted in York-Scarborough and 45,000 in Vancouver Centre, while only 18,000 went to the polls in Meadow Lake, Saskatchewan, and 19,000 in Gaspé, Quebec.

Recent reforms in Ontario and British Columbia have removed some of the worst imbalances in those provinces. Yet even after a thorough-going redistribution of seats in Ontario in 1966, the population in the constituencies ranged from 30,000 to over 70,000, and Metropolitan Toronto elected only 26 of the 117 members of the legislature although it had almost one-quarter of the province's population. British Columbia also carried out a major redistribution in 1966. But Greater Vancouver, with half the provincial population, still sent only 23 of the 55 members to Victoria. In Atlin only 1200 people voted, while the number of voters in city municipalities often reached 20,000.

It would be relatively easy to make every constituency contain an equal number of voters. The opponents of equal representation raise two arguments against it. The rural citizen, they argue, is likely to be a property owner, a man whose personal roots, like those of his crops, lie deep in the soil of the country. Having a greater stake in the community, the argument runs, he will take his political duties more seriously than the rootless wage earner of the city. Decades ago, before Canada was urbanized and industrialized, this argument may have carried weight. It hardly does so today.

The second argument is stronger. If all ridings were equal in population, some rural ridings would be enormous in size. The Member of Parliament would find it difficult, if not impossible, to travel throughout the constituency to familiarize himself with his constituents and their problems. Government would be even further removed from the people.

Government by Majority

Most Canadians accept the principle that in a democracy there should be government by a majority, or majority rule. Once again a glance beneath the surface reveals a gap between principle and practice, for it has often happened in Canada and elsewhere that the government represents the choice of fewer than half the voters who went to the polls. Moreover, party strength in the House of Commons often bears little relation to the votes received. How this happens can be easily explained.

Imagine for a moment that in each constituency only two candidates, a Liberal and a Conservative, are running. The voting could be such that in every constituency the Liberal candidate got only one vote less than the Conservative. The Liberals would win no seats and the Conservatives, with a total of only two hundred and sixty-four votes more than the Liberals, would hold every seat in the House of Commons. This, of course, is absurd. But seats have been won by one vote, and a margin of one vote is as good as one of ten thousand in winning an election.

Moreover, the existence of three, four or even five parties running candidates in an election causes further distortions. With the vote split many ways the winner often

receives fewer than half the votes. (It might cause a visitor
from a non-democratic state to question some democratic
principles when he saw a man representing a constituency
in which 70 per cent of the people voted against him!)
In short, as a result of these aspects of our democratic
system, it is possible that the number of seats held by a
party in the House of Commons may not fairly reflect its
popular strength. Table 1, showing the percentage of the
total votes received and the seats held in some recent national elections, reveals the discrepancies clearly. Since
1921 only one government in Canada, the Conservative
government elected in 1958, has represented more than
half the Canadian voters.

TABLE 1

	Liberals		Conservatives		C.C.F. & N.D.P.		S.C.	
	%	%	%	%	%	%	%	%
Year	Votes	Seats	Votes	Seats	Votes	Seats	Votes	Seats
1935	46	72	30	16	9	3	4	8
1945	41	51	28	26	16	11	4	5
1953	50	65	31	19	11	9	5	6
1958	33	18	54	79	10	3	2	0
1962	37	38	37	44	13	7	12	11
1963	41	49	33	36	14	6	12	9
1965	40	49	32	37	18	8	9	5
1968	45	59	31	27	17	8	6	6

The Parliament elected in 1958 illustrates another pecu-
liarity in our representative system. On a rough estimate,
every Conservative Member represented 18,000 voters, every
Liberal represented 49,000, every C.C.F. Member 80,000.
Though the Liberal and C.C.F. Parties found this a
deplorable situation, they were much better off than the
Social Credit Party, whose voters after the election of 1958
were unrepresented in the House of Commons. In 1968

the figures were not as dramatic, with each Liberal representing about 23,000, the Conservatives about 34,000 and
the N.D.P. 64,000.

So far we have used the national, or federal, Parliament
as our example in discussing our system of representation
and its peculiarities. The same system and the same flaws
exist in the provinces. The figures in Table 2 for the 1963
and 1967 provincial elections in Ontario need no further
comment, although the improvements after the 1966 redistribution are obvious.

TABLE 2

Party	% Total Vote		% Seats	
	1963	1967	1963	1967
Conservatives	48	42	71	59
Liberals	35	31	22	24
N.D.P.	16	25	6	17
Other	1	2	—	—

The 1969 election in British Columbia gave the Social
Credit Party 69 per cent of the seats with 47 per cent of the
vote, while the N.D.P. and the Liberals won 21 and 9
per cent of the seats with 34 and 19 per cent of the
popular vote respectively.

A Solution?

Most people agree that the weaknesses so clearly observ-
able in our representative system demand some solution.
But no one can find a remedy which satisfies everyone, or
which does not raise as many problems as it solves. Some
have favoured the creation of electoral districts with equal
population and have been heartened by the redistributions
mentioned earlier. Others have advocated a system in
which the voter lists the candidates in order of his pref-
erence. This system, known as the transferable vote, has
been tried in Manitoba's rural seats and in British
Columbia without much success.

The most commonly proffered solution is proportional representation. Ideally, with proportional representation the seats held in the legislature would be in proportion to the votes gained in the election. Using the figures for the Ontario election of 1967 in Table 2, the present condition would compare with that under proportional representation as follows:

TABLE 3

Party	Seats Held	Seats Under Proportional Representation
Conservatives	69	49+
Liberals	28	37+
N.D.P.	20	29+

While proportional representation would make for a fairer distribution of seats it also raises one major problem. The Ontario election of 1967 did give the Conservatives a clear majority of seats, thus enabling the government to pass its legislation in the Assembly. With proportional representation, however, it would not have had a majority and would have had to depend on the support of either the Liberals or the N.D.P.

Such "minority governments," as we call them, sometimes occur under the present system of representation and are often unstable and ineffective. Mr. Diefenbaker led a minority government after the election of June 18, 1962, but it only lasted until February 1963. The ensuing election on April 8 returned Mr. Pearson and the Liberals but once again without a clear majority of seats. Two years later, following intense pressure from within his own party, Mr. Pearson went to the people again, asking for a clear majority. A minority government, he argued, could not effectively get legislation through Parliament. The electorate was unconvinced, however, and on November 8, while

"BY THE WAY, MY RESIGNATION IS IN MY DESK DRAWER UNDER THE BASEBALL MITT"

Mr. Pearson in search of a majority in 1965.

the Liberals were returned to power, they won only 131 of the 265 seats.

Some people have argued that minority governments are healthy. The government, they maintain, is forced to listen to the views of the opposition parties, since a united opposition could defeat it. Moreover, dependent on other parties for support in the House of Commons, it must develop policies and legislation which have an appeal to people representing a wider range in the political spectrum. However, it is unlikely that a majority of Canadians would favour any change in the representative system that would make minority governments a permanent feature of Canadian government, because minority governments are unstable. Likely to be defeated at any moment, the government is constantly thinking of an election, as are the opposition parties. The political atmosphere is thus not the most ideal for a systematic approach to the nation's problems or the calm and orderly discussion of public affairs.

Even if our governments always had the support of a majority of Canadians, there could still be problems. Simple majority rule does not ensure satisfactory government, for a majority might use its power like a dictator or absolute monarch to tyrannize the rest of the people. Dictatorship by a group is no more acceptable than dictatorship by an individual. Canadians believe that in addition to majority rule, democratic government demands protection for the rights of minorities. Among the most important of these rights are freedom of speech, press and association, and freedom from arbitrary arrest. With such civil rights or liberties guaranteed, it is possible for a minority peacefully to make itself a majority.

In a comparatively homogeneous nation like Britain this concept of democracy—majority rule plus individual civil rights—satisfies most citizens. Canada, however, is a pluralistic country composed of people of many different racial and cultural backgrounds. In addition to the Indians and Eskimos and the English and French founding races, there are such ethnic groups as Ukrainians, Poles, Germans, Italians and many others, who collectively make up about 25 per cent of the population. In the United States such groups have been closely woven into the fabric of American society. In Canada ethnic groups have been more inclined to remain in geographic and cultural isolation, retaining to a far greater extent the ways of their homelands. Some spokesmen for ethnic groups argue that individual civil rights do not provide sufficient safeguards to maintain the group culture.

By far the most serious problem in this connection centres around the French Canadians, many of whom completely reject the idea of majority rule as a satisfactory political basis in Canada. History has taught French Canada that when issues unite the rest of the country, majority rule can be a tyranny from which the existence of individual freedoms can provide no relief. French Canadians regard Confederation as a compact which guaranteed them equality of status and opportunity in a bicultural state. Instead, because the rest of Canada—the majority—refuse to accept this concept, the French Canadian can be French only in Quebec. Speaking before the Royal Commission on Bilingualism and Biculturalism, a Quebec lawyer described French-speaking Canada as ". . . a cohesive minority society with a long history of political, economic and cultural domination by a majority society. . . . When they speak of equality English Canadians mean equality of individual civil rights, that is, of persons considered individually, while when we French Canadians speak of equality we do not mean civil rights at all, we mean collective national rights, we mean the rights of the French Canadian nation to develop in accordance with its own characteristics. . . ." As a result many French Canadians have come to endorse the idea of a double majority—one English and one French—with French Canada possessing the status of an associate state in the Canadian federation.

How We Vote: Electoral Machinery

The chart on page 23 shows clearly how the elaborate machinery functions throughout an election from the time the decision is made to hold an election until the votes are counted and the victors announced. Every step in this procedure is designed to guarantee the fairest, most honest and most efficient election. The present system is not the result of a sudden plan but of a hundred years of experiment and experiences. To look back over that development might help us understand why today's practices take the form they do.

Nominations

At the present time, nominations of candidates are usually presented formally in petitions signed by ten citizens in the constituency. The person nominated must deposit two hundred dollars as a proof of his serious intention to run for Parliament. Both practices were introduced in 1874 by the Liberal government led by Alexander Mackenzie. Before 1874, nominations were held on hustings, or platforms, in the open air, and after the nominations the candidates would address the people. Nomination day was colourful and exciting, sometimes too exciting. When Sir John A. Macdonald, the Prime Minister, was nominated as a candidate for Kingston, Ontario, in 1872, the crowd's exuberance was boundless. When the candidates attempted to speak, they were constantly interrupted by shouts and yells. Fistfights occurred at frequent intervals among the spectators. Even the two candidates lost their tempers and engaged in a free-for-all on the platform.

In Kamouraska, Quebec, an unpopular election official described his experiences on nomination day:

> When I had ascended the gallery . . . one Pierre Lafrance, a navigator from St. Anne, snatched from my hands the election law, and immediately afterwards I was precipitated from the gallery by Thomas LeBel, farmer, and Michel LeBel, formerly a trader, both of St. Louis de Kamouraska, the former seizing me by the legs, and the latter throwing himself upon me. . . . I had not sufficient force to resist the acts of violence committed on my person . . . and I had been able to procure no more than eight constables, who were more disposed to provide for their own safety than to remain where they were; moreover, it would have required an armed force to keep the peace, and to enable me to hold my ground; and I really apprehended danger to my life.

In one constituency, the Liberals complained that the Returning Officer was conveniently deaf when the Liberal nomination was made, so deaf in fact that the Conservative candidate was elected by acclamation. On another occasion the official was supposed to have held the nomination proceedings in the woods. No one objected to the location, but some wished he had informed more than one party of his intention!

Mackenzie's reforms, to which there was some opposi-

THE PLANNING OF AN ELECTION

1. The Prime Minister decides to hold an election and advises the Governor-General. From the Governor-General, who acts on the Prime Minister's advice, an order goes to the Chief Electoral Officer, the civil servant in charge of the election machinery, to put the machine in motion.

2. The Chief Electoral Officer sends out to the Returning Officer, the official responsible for the election in each constituency, instructions to publish the dates for nomination of candidates and voting. The Returning Officer divides the constituency into polling stations, or voting locations, one for every 300 voters.

3. The Returning Officer has a list made up and published of all people entitled to vote.

4. Each party nominates its candidate and informs the Returning Officer of its choice by filing nomination papers with him. Anyone can be a candidate if he is a Canadian citizen or a British subject, twenty-one years of age or over and deposits $200 to show that he is serious. The deposit is returned if the candidate receives half as many votes as the winner.

5. On election day the polls, each supervised by a Deputy Returning Officer, are open from 8 a.m. to 7 p.m. (standard time). The voter enters the polling station, gives his name and receives a ballot which he marks secretly and hands to the Deputy Returning Officer who places it in a box. After 7 p.m. the boxes are opened and the ballots counted. By midnight the results are usually fairly well decided in favour of one candidate.

tion in the House of Commons, did not prevent irregularities, but these became exceptional. The system of nomination has remained substantially the same since 1874.

The Secret Ballot

In 1867 when the Canadian nation was formed, voting was carried on in the open by word of mouth or by a show of hands. The system was open to many abuses, the most common of which was intimidation. Employers were inclined to look with disfavour upon employees who did not see politics in the right light, that is, as the employers saw it. Fathers often looked upon sons in the same way. Gangs of toughs made life unpleasant for men brave enough to stand by their opinions, and priests and ministers sometimes felt strongly enough about an election to exercise influence that bordered on coercion in persuading their parishioners to vote as their religious advisers wished.

To lessen the threat of intimidation, and to increase the voter's freedom of choice, the Mackenzie government introduced the secret ballot in 1874, just two years after Prime Minister Gladstone had done so in England. In both countries there was strong opposition to the change from open to secret voting. Some felt that no man should be ashamed of his political beliefs. That may well have been what Sir John A. Macdonald meant when he said that voting in secret was "un-British." But shame and fear, as Macdonald must have known, are very different things. More honest, if not more common, was the frank admission that the secret ballot would cut at the root of political corruption—the open or secret bribing of the voters. Before the secret ballot was introduced, candidates knew what a vote was worth in any given area, and some voters held out for a high price, whether it was in cash or merchandise. With a secret ballot how was one to know if the bribed man had voted as he had promised? As Premier Norquay of Manitoba argued, the secret ballot "encourages immorality and duplicity." But even Norquay was forced to consent and Manitoba got the secret ballot in 1888.

Typical of the widespread corruption was the election in West Hastings, Ontario, in 1878. William Sarsfield was one of the many witnesses who later appeared before a judge to give evidence on oath of his part during the election. Sarsfield worked for the Conservative candidate, a Mr. Robertson, who won the election but was later unseated for corrupt practices. Sarsfield told the court:

> I used all my influence for Robertson. I tried to get a man named Maloney to vote. I used every induce-ment to get him to vote. I gave him $1 and got it back. I suppose it was not enough money for his vote. . . . I gave T. Harris 50¢ to try to get him to vote for Robertson; I promised him $2 more. He got $1.85 and three drinks. I had $40 to $45 in my pocket that morning. . . . I spent some of my money that day; I can't say how much. I paid people money to go and vote for Robertson. . . . I can't say how many I paid after the election.

This case, in fact, was heard after the secret ballot had been introduced. Sarsfield had to trust those whom he bribed, but in the bad old days of public voting one could be more certain that a man would not take the bribe and then vote the other way.

Practices such as those engaged in by Sarsfield still ex-isted early in the present century and undoubtedly exist from time to time in various elections today. Describing an election in Quebec early in the century, Senator C. G. "Chubby" Power has written in his memoirs:

> Ample evidences of the candidate's great generosity were not lacking. Tons of coal, baskets of groceries and other luxuries and necessities appeared as by magic in the homes. On our side, tavern-keepers, those ever-im-portant shapers of public opinion, were handsomely subsidized to exert their powerful influence in the late hours of the evening. At great length and in inspired accents, they lauded the qualifications of 'Laurier's bosom friend' [Power]. . . .
> Then there were the groups of 'wavering' voters who organized themselves into clubs. The 'supplies' for these clubs were furnished by both parties; and it was pos-

sible to spend an evening dancing and drinking with an interval during which the waverers allowed themselves to be momentarily swayed by speakers from one side or the other. . . . The gospel was spread on both sides in the most unholy manner. With liquor and money so widely and evenly distributed, the issues so eloquently and inspiringly expounded and so clearly understood, the election was bound to be close, and it was.

In addition to all this, election day was a pretty costly business. There were first the 'faithful' supporters who not only expected but demanded concrete rewards for casting their votes. Then there were those shrewder fellows who realized that votes were an asset not to be disposed of lightly and who solicited 'bid and raise' with all the cunning of a capable auctioneer before they cast a ballot.*

The decision to use the secret ballot raised a problem. Unless the actual form of the ballot could not be easily copied, there was nothing to prevent unscrupulous candidates from printing their own ballots and "stuffing" the boxes with them. As late as 1900, the government was still trying to solve the problem and in that year ordered the name of the printer to be clearly indicated on the ballot. Since it was known how many ballots came from each printer, false ballots could be readily detected. Even this simple precaution had its defects, however, for one printer took the order so seriously and printed his name so prominently that a good many votes were cast for him.

The present form of ballot, reproduced opposite, is extremely effective. Simple as it is, it still succeeds in baffling a small but determined group of Canadians— 60,000 in 1962—who every election spoil their ballots by marking them incorrectly. The name of the party to which a candidate belongs cannot be printed on the ballot. It has been suggested that a photograph of each candidate be run beside his name to help the voter identify the various contestants.

*Excerpt from *A Party Politician: The Memoirs of Chubby Power*, edited by Norman Ward, reprinted by permission of the Macmillan Company of Canada Limited.

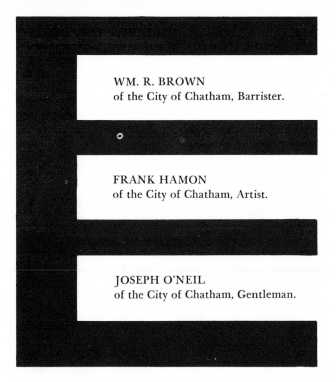

WM. R. BROWN
of the City of Chatham, Barrister.

FRANK HAMON
of the City of Chatham, Artist.

JOSEPH O'NEIL
of the City of Chatham, Gentleman.

Election Expenses

Bribery and other corrupt practices have always been difficult to define and stamp out. The cynic might suggest that there is little difference between a gift or a payment in cash and the promise of a new road, a post office or employment on some public project. But the only workable definition of bribery has been one that involved a direct payment to an individual to vote in a certain way.

Bribery used to be such a common practice that one judge asked in all seriousness whether it was not really "the cornerstone of Party Government" and wondered how political parties could be victorious without wholesale bribery of the electorate. That everyone broke the law was almost taken for granted. For example, one-third of the Members elected to the House of Commons in 1874 were later unseated for corrupt practices.

Legislation first introduced by the Liberals in 1874 demanded that every candidate keep a record of his expenses and make it public. The law is still in force, but has never really been effective. One Member of Parliament candidly declared in the Commons, "I think it quite a stretch of credulity to imagine that anyone who is so wickedly inclined as to commit a corrupt practice is going to write

The promise of a causeway to Prince Edward Island has always indicated that an election cannot be far away. Before the 1965 election Prime Minister Pearson promised the causeway, and the **Toronto Star's** Duncan Macpherson played the cynic. The Islanders, too, were cynics—some of them simply did not want to be united to the mainland—and returned a full contingent of Conservatives.

down on paper that he did so." Professor Norman Ward, author of *The Canadian House of Commons*, has written that the Members of Parliament are more inclined "to accept accusations of unscrupulousness than of stupidity." All experts agree that the published statements and the real expenses of candidates are worlds apart. Candidates who have listed only three thousand dollars as expenses have later admitted that it cost between ten thousand and fifty thousand dollars to run an election in their constituency, and some have stated that an expenditure of one hundred thousand dollars was not unusual. Newspaper advertisements, costly television appearances, posters and postcards, committee rooms and party workers make an election too expensive for the ordinary candidate. He thus becomes dependent on party headquarters for money. The party, in turn, has to look far and wide for financial support, for an adequate election fund might run to millions of dollars.

The time has come to consider political parties, for they are the life-blood of the Canadian governmental system.

3 POLITICAL PARTIES

Political parties in a democracy like Canada with universal suffrage are a necessary means of organizing us to govern ourselves. Political parties are like magnets. They should gather the millions of voters around two or more poles. To attract the voters, each party takes a stand on matters affecting the nation, whether they be economic, political, cultural or international affairs. The parties put their platforms before the voters, who then gravitate into the magnetic field of the party whose ideas attract them most—or repel them least. The voter does not necessarily agree with everything any one party stands for, but he usually finds less fault with Party A than with Party B. The party, in turn, anxious to attract as many people as possible, uses its programme or platform, its selection of a leader and its choice of candidates to build up its magnetic field.

Democracy and representative government, as we understand them, would be impossible without political parties. Imagine for a moment our system without parties. Who would pick candidates? And when the candidates were elected, would enough of them agree on public questions to have a majority in the legislature? Would the members be able to concur in the choice of a leader? Would they be able to settle on one solution for every problem that arose, or would each member cling to his own theory? And if they did manage to agree on the solution, would there be a consensus on the best way to put it into effect? It is likely that decision and action would be almost impossible without some form of party government. In Canada, political parties help to make the difference between order and chaos in government (although the difference may sometimes seem slight).

We have compared political parties to magnets. Edmund

THE BALLOTEERS

Burke, the eighteenth-century philosopher-politician, once defined a political party as a "body of men united for promoting the national interest on some particular principle on which they are all agreed." In Burke's view a party was the embodiment of an idea, or a series of ideas or principles. At various times in Canada (as also in Great Britain and the United States) Burke's definition would have been appropriate. Usually, however, there are many issues, none of them clear-cut, and party principles are difficult to formulate. We might, therefore, reword Burke's definition to conform to the contemporary situation. It might read "a body of men who share a general point of view towards public questions."

Principles or Power?

Ideally, political parties should organize the voters on the basis of principles or points of view towards public affairs. The clearer their policies, the clearer and more logical is the voter's mind and choice. Historically, parties have served the purpose of clarifying issues and offering alternative programmes. In nineteenth-century England, Liberals and Conservatives represented two general points of view, two political philosophies and programmes. Gladstone and the Liberals emphasized individual rights and individual freedom. Disraeli and the Conservatives dwelt more on society's needs. The Liberals drew firm support from the urban middle class and tended to speak for them, while the Conservatives relied for power on the country squire and voiced his interests. After the city labourer secured the vote in 1867 and 1884, a new Labour Party emerged to represent him in politics and to plead the case for social welfare and reform.

In Canada there was similarly a marked difference between the parties in the nineteenth century. Conservatives in the days of Sir John A. Macdonald concentrated on the economic development of Canada and looked with fear upon the United States. They sought and gained the alliance of the businessmen. Liberals more truly represented the farmers. They had less fear of the threat to Canada's independence posed by the United States and were more concerned about emancipating the new nation from domination and control by Britain. Splinter parties like the short-lived Progressives and the Co-operative Commonwealth Federation (C.C.F.) sprang up in the twentieth century to voice the demands of farmers and workingmen when it became apparent that both major parties were neglecting to do so.

Yet we know that today party principles are often obscure, vague and uncertain, and that at times it is difficult to distinguish the ideas of one party from those of the others. Why is this?

Platform and Policies

The aim of a political party is to win power. Without power it achieves nothing. Within every party there are those who genuinely believe that they can improve the country and there are those, unfortunately, who seek power only for its own sake. Whatever the motive, the fact remains that the primary object of a party is to get into office. To do this, it must win more seats in the House of Commons than any other party.

Every party, therefore, attempts to have something to offer everybody. It usually seeks to make a general rather than a particular appeal, to have as broad and flexible a point of view as possible. It tries to attract people in all walks of life, of all religious and racial backgrounds, in all regions and provinces. In a country as vast and diversified as Canada, this is not an easy task. The interests of the Nova Scotia fisherman, the Ontario factory-worker, the Quebec grocer, the prairie farmer and the British Columbia logger are not only dissimilar, they are often conflicting. Stockbrokers and steelworkers, old Canadians and new, Roman Catholics and Protestants may often look at issues with different eyes. Yet the political party seeks to appeal to all of these voters; it tries to be, if not all things to all men, at least a good many things to a good many men. As a result, it often does not pay a party to define its policy too clearly, lest what attracts the farmer may alienate the doctor. Parties often tend to be more critical of their opponents than anxious to make their own positions clear. They advocate peace and prosperity, honesty in government, or "two cars in every garage and a chicken in every pot." Broad generalizations like these are too often a substitute for clear and concise statements of policy.

As a result, it is frequently very difficult to distinguish

Although Arch Dale was hitting out at his favourite target, the Conservative leader, R. B. Bennett, in this cartoon of the election of 1930, political parties too often make an election appeal which sounds very much like "If you don't see what you want ask for it."

one party from another. Although each party may have a fixed body of supporters, it must compete with the other parties for the vote of the uncommitted, and defeat or victory will depend on its success in doing so. To appeal to any given body of uncommitted voters, every party usually will say much the same thing, and usually what the voter wants to hear.

In defence of the politicians, however, it must be said that the voters are often as unclear as the party platforms.

Today there are few Canadians who do not advocate
strenuous efforts to control pollution, to protect the economy and culture of the country against increasing American
domination, and to improve the standard of living for the
poor, the unemployed, and the unfortunate. But when
debate turns from the desired goals to the means necessary
to achieve them unanimity ends. How much government
direction or control? How much higher personal taxes?
What decline in capital investment can be tolerated? What
level of income and for precisely what types of people?
For the voter as for the party, political decisions involve
many trade-offs. Unless taxes are raised no additional
funds can be spent. If they are raised, should the money be
spent on education, highways, pollution control, buying
back the economy, raising income levels for the poor, or
subsidizing athletics? Each decision is a matter of judge-
ment; there is no monopoly on truth or wisdom. What is
not true is the politician's favourite campaign promise that
public spending can be increased and public taxes lowered.

It is not only the complexity of issues and the wariness
of a political party about losing support of important
groups or regions that encourage parties to sound much
alike. There is also a general agreement among Canadian
voters—or Americans or British for that matter—on many
issues. While all Canadians object to higher taxes, most of
us accept the general idea of the welfare state. Some complain that the pace of reform is too slow or too fast, and
the taxes to support health and welfare too heavy on them
or their company. But the view that the state should in
some way protect its citizens against starvation or mal-
nutrition, sickness and disease is widely shared. As public
opinion has shifted, the Liberals and Conservatives have
become more socialistic and have been willing to move
further and faster than they would have ten or twenty years
ago. Socialists have become more moderate, or have seemed
to as some of their goals have been realized, and have
learned that it does not pay politically to be too far in
advance of public opinion.

For example, the C.C.F. Party, formed in 1932, had a

One of the leading members of WAFFLE is Mel Watkins, a University of Toronto Professor and author of the Watkins Report on foreign ownership of Canadian industry. WAFFLE proposes a highly nationalistic programme of preventing foreign ownership and taking over American corporations in Canada as an essential step towards a socialist state.

definite and clearly defined socialist platform that involved socialization, or government ownership, of banks, insurance companies, transportation, power, and important industries. But the platform was too radical for most voters, and years of defeat at the polls forced the C.C.F. to desert many of its original principles in an attempt to attract more voters. Finally, in 1961, it was submerged in the New Democratic Party (N.D.P.) whose platform, while left of centre, is closer to that of the major parties. Yet the old socialist element has remained, and in recent years has found a new expression in the WAFFLE group, a young element in the party that advocates a return to undiluted socialism and a vigorous nationalism for the party. As they fight off the challenge from WAFFLE, the N.D.P. leaders repeatedly argue that such a radical platform may be fine in principle, but is not the way to political power.

In short, in their attempts to win the broadest measure of support from all classes of people and all sections of the country, political parties tend to gravitate toward the middle of the road. And whenever possible they seek to force their opponents into the ditch on either the left or the right by portraying them as either radicals or reactionaries.

Once a party has won solid support in an election through its middle-of-the-road policies, it is very difficult to dislodge. With a sure footing, it is in a good position to withstand its rivals: it chooses the time of the next election, has government favours to bestow, generally selects the campaign issues on favourable territory and can, through legislation before the election, secure the support of doubtful groups of voters. In fact, it is usually only when some major or unexpected issue arises, or when the party leadership changes, that governments lose elections. The Conservatives governed Canada from 1878 to 1896, the Liberals from 1896 to 1911, and again from 1935 to 1957. The Liberals ruled without defeat in Ontario from 1871 to 1905, in Quebec from 1897 to 1936, and in Nova Scotia from 1882 to 1925—forty-three years without a defeat. Until recently at least, James Russell Lowell's verse,

> He stood a spell on one foot fust,
> Then stood a spell on t'other,
> An' on which one he felt the wust
> He couldn't ha' told ye nuther,

could hardly be considered true for Canada, unless we say "long spell."

The search for power, then, often conflicts with the firm adherence to principles or clear policies, or at least waters them down. Yet to speak of politics or government in terms other than of power is unreal. At the same time, power should not be an end in itself. There must be a compromise between principles and power. It is the task of the citizen to make certain that principles are not sacrificed on the altar of power. With his vote he is able to punish when punishment is due.

Organization

Politicians have been heard to remark that in winning elections ideas and policies are about as helpful as fairy-tales. A few good rousing war-cries are useful, but party organization or "the machine" is what wins elections. As Israel Tarte, a veteran Quebec politician who had fought and won elections for thirty years, wryly observed at the dawn of the twentieth century, "Elections are not won with prayers."

Party organization is a ladder with the rungs reaching from the individual party members up to the party chieftains. The bottom rung is the local poll association and above it are the constituency organizations, the regional or provincial associations and finally the national headquarters. On all levels, except the poll association, there are women's groups, young people's clubs, study groups and inner circles. Between elections the entire organization generally runs in low gear and on some levels, particularly that of the polling area, stops completely. But as soon as the first whisper of an election comes from or to party headquarters, the machine moves quickly into high gear.

The members of the organization who come into direct contact with the voters are those belonging to the local poll or constituency. Before an election they canvass the area, door by door, distributing literature, attempting to persuade the doubtful and identify the party adherents. On election day they watch at the polling stations and, as closing-time approaches, telephone those who have not voted and might vote for their party to remind them of their duty. Sometimes transportation or the services of baby-sitters are offered to get voters to the polls. In other words, these political workers "get out the vote." Provincial or national headquarters, depending on the election, prepares the over-all campaign programme, arranges for guest speakers, and radio and T.V. programmes and provides the bulk of the campaign funds or party war chest.

National elections cost the large parties millions of dollars for printing expenses, transportation, broadcasts and the renting of offices and halls. A small portion of the money comes from the ordinary party member who may

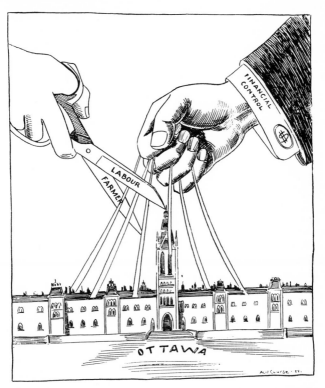

The caption on this cartoon, which appeared in the Winnipeg **Weekly News** in 1925, read: "Free the Country and Industry from the Hand of Invisible Government." The cartoonist quoted the Progressive Member, Mr. Good, with approval: "If we do not have public control over finances, we are going to have control of the public by financiers. We can take our choice." Implicit in the farmer-labour alliance was the belief that the Liberals and Conservatives were under the control of the big business and financial interests.

contribute as he would to a club. Much more comes from the wealthy members of the party who are solicited for substantial sums. But probably the bulk of it comes from the people in industry and business who want the government to look kindly towards them from time to time. Large manufacturing concerns, for example, hope that their views will be favourably looked on whenever a revision of the tariff is considered, for they know that if the tariff is lowered on foreign goods of the kind they produce, their profits will fall or their businesses fail. Sir John A. Macdonald once compared these men who seek government aid to a man who said of whiskey that "a little too much is just enough."

Often such contributions are made to more than one political party, and sometimes, in an attempt to defeat the government, wealthy corporations or individuals invest heavily in an opposition party, particularly if it seems that the opposition might win the election. On the whole, however, the government of the day finds it easier than its opponents to raise money, and its war chest, as a result, is richer. On this point there is no better authority than Prime Minister R. B. Bennett, who once told the House of Commons:

> Anyone who knows anything about campaign funds knows the party in power is always able to obtain them with readiness as compared with anybody else, for the contributions that are made, not for corrupt purposes but for purposes of enabling the organization of the party to be effective, are made on the assumption that the party in power is best able to attend to affairs because it has power to do great injury to those who are carrying on the business in this country.

The Prime Minister might have added "great assistance" as well as "great injury." He might also have said "not *necessarily* for corrupt purposes," for the record reveals, time and time again, that such donations have been made to secure specific favours from the government and that sometimes the favour depended on the gift. The most notorious case of this kind occurred during the election of 1872 when Sir John A. Macdonald's Conservative Party accepted more than a quarter of a million dollars from a man who wished to secure a contract to build the Canadian Pacific Railway. When the facts of this "Pacific Scandal" were revealed Macdonald resigned rather than face defeat in the Commons or dismissal by the Governor-General. In the 1920's Mackenzie King's Liberal Party received seven hundred thousand dollars from people interested in developing the St. Lawrence hydro-electric power system. Actually the donors had already secured their demands, but they maintained that "gratefulness was always regarded as an important factor in dealing with democratic government."

There is no doubt that reliance on outside sources for large party war chests makes the politicians and the party vulnerable—or at least provides the appearance of vulnerability. In 1964, for example, it was widely suggested that the difficulty experienced by the government in finding Hal Banks had something to do with alleged contributions to the Liberal Party in the past. A suspicious public was also ready to believe that Lucien Rivard's escape from a Montreal jail (engineered on the pretext that he wanted to water the skating rink on a balmy night) was related to party contributions. On the other hand, there may be situations which provide ample ground for the public's suspicion. It was quite clear, for example, that Rivard's friends, who wanted to prevent his extradition to the United States to face charges of peddling narcotics, assumed that some politicians would be more co-operative if they could expect political contributions in return.

Only by freeing the individual politician and the party from their need for funds will the dangers of corruption diminish substantially. The most hopeful modern solution to an age-old problem has come from Quebec, where the past record has been among the worst in Canada. In 1963 the Lesage government passed an act limiting election expenses and providing for partial reimbursement by the state. Put into effect for the first time during the 1966 provincial election, the law limits every candidate to spending sixty cents for each voter up to a limit of 10,000 voters, plus fifty cents for those between 10,000 and 20,000, and forty cents for each voter over 20,000. In constituencies where the population is spread over an unusually large area, however, the candidate may spend an additional ten cents for each voter. The law also provides for reimburse-

The great nineteenth-century cartoonist, J. Bengough, unleashed a volley at Sir John A. Macdonald in 1873 following the revelation of the Pacific Scandal. Ninety-two years later, when rumours, reports and facts concerning corruption in Ottawa were made public, cartoonist Macpherson could not resist the temptation.

ment by the government of fifteen cents for each elector, with an increment of between one and seven cents a voter in constituencies with over 10,000 voters. Each candidate must file a statement of expenses with the Chief Electoral Officer. To receive reimbursement he must belong to a recognized political party which ran at least ten candidates and he must have won at least 20 per cent of the vote in his constituency.

The Quebec law is far from adequate, let alone perfect. The largest portion of allowable election expenses must still be met either by the candidate or the party, and it may be difficult to enforce the limitation. Party headquarters are neither limited in, nor reimbursed for, their expenses in the production of literature, radio and T.V. advertising, travelling or a host of other costs in the election campaign, much less for the immense cost of keeping the party going between elections.

Nevertheless, the Quebec law provides a beginning. Nova Scotia passed similar legislation in 1969, and in 1970 a Commons committee recommended that the Canadian government adopt a comparable practice.

Party Leadership

It would be interesting and enlightening to ask a thousand voters what they voted for in the last provincial or national election. It is quite likely that we should find the majority of them voted not for a party as such, nor for a policy, but for or against a man. In isolated cases the voter might have cast his ballot for the local candidate, but generally it would be for the party leader. It is he who must not only manage his Cabinet and his party with great dexterity to hold together the diversity of groups and interests which make up the country, but who must also somehow become the party's symbol. Canadians, then, often choose their Prime Minister by going to the polls and voting for the local candidate of the same party.

This is of immense importance. What the voter may really be doing, in other words, is electing the executive and in so doing also electing the legislature; for as we shall see later the Prime Minister is chosen because he has more followers in the House of Commons than the leaders of the other parties. Moreover, because we vote for the Prime Minister, who is the practical head of the executive, the executive exercises very great power over the legislature.

At this point, however, we should realize only that the party leader is perhaps the most important figure in Canadian politics. The qualities he must possess are many and varied, and very few men have satisfied all the requirements. Those who do are likely to remain in office for a long time. This is not to say that every leader must have the same qualities. At first sight the jovial, down-to-earth Macdonald, the warm, dignified Laurier and the aloof, cautious King seem to have had little in common. Yet beneath the surface they all had, in varying degrees, an unusual ability to sense the common mood, a way with men, a willingness to compromise when necessary, a nerve as cool as ice-water—in all, an acute political sense that defies definition.

Without an adequate leader, a political party is doomed to rest forever in the shades of opposition just as the national Conservative Party did for over twenty years. During this time it was often remarked that the Conservative leader was the Liberals' chief political asset. The Conservative Party changed leaders five times before finding in John Diefenbaker a man who could win an election.

The Liberals had high hopes for Lester B. Pearson, the brilliant diplomat, when he succeeded Louis St. Laurent after the 1957 election. But Mr. Pearson's talents in diplomacy were not easily transferred to the public arena or the T.V. screen, and the quiet diplomacy of external affairs was a far cry from the rough and tumble of politics. Under Mr. Pearson the Liberals lost the elections of 1958 and 1962, managed to defeat a tottering Conservative government in 1963, and retained a slim lead in 1965. But when Pierre Elliott Trudeau was elected leader in 1968 Liberal fortunes changed overnight. After only a few weeks as Prime Minister, Trudeau called an election. The dashing bachelor, fluent in two languages, skilled on the diving board and the motorcycle, forthright and sophisticated,

"Mr. Prime Minister, are you absolutely sure you didn't make any promises during the election campaign?"

evoked some magnetic response in the electorate. What reporters soon called Trudeaumania swept the country, and the Liberals coasted to an overwhelming victory on the Prime Minister's charm.

Having discussed our representative system, with its virtues and weaknesses, the time has come to move on to a consideration of our parliamentary system to determine the framework in which Canadian politics operate.

4 THE CANADIAN PARLIAMENTARY SYSTEM

The British North America Act of 1867, which created the Dominion of Canada, laid down the structure of our government in words which, even then, described the traditional outward form rather than the real inner workings of the system of parliamentary government already in use in the British North American colonies. When the real facts that lie behind these words are understood, one has a picture of our whole parliamentary system of government.

At the head of Canada's government is the Queen. She is chief of the executive and is a part of Parliament. In Canada she is represented by the Governor-General. Advising the Governor-General is the Privy Council whose members, the Act says, are appointed and may be removed by the Governor-General. But this is the form only, and not the true substance of the relationship between the Governor-General and his advisers. The several colonies of British North America had had, and the new Dominion of Canada inherited, "a constitution similar in principle to that of the United Kingdom." This meant that in fact the Crown (the Governor-General) would act on the advice of a group of ministers who were answerable, in turn, to the House of Commons. This group is the Cabinet and is made up of the Prime Minister and the other men currently serving with him as ministers of the Crown. Every person who serves as a minister of the Crown becomes a Privy Councillor and remains one for the rest of his life. Custom dictates that only those privy councillors who are members of the current Cabinet take any part in advising the Governor-General. The Cabinet is the active part of the Privy Council. You will not find in the British North America Act any mention of the Cabinet as such, nor of the Prime Minister, although they are the real centre of power under the British system of government. They are

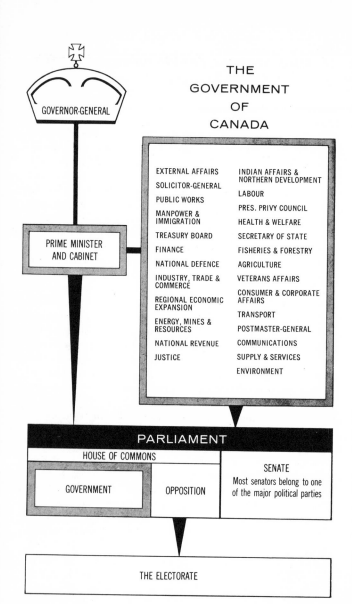

THE
GOVERNMENT
OF
CANADA

GOVERNOR-GENERAL

PRIME MINISTER
AND CABINET

EXTERNAL AFFAIRS

SOLICITOR-GENERAL

PUBLIC WORKS

MANPOWER &
IMMIGRATION

TREASURY BOARD

FINANCE

NATIONAL DEFENCE

INDUSTRY, TRADE &
COMMERCE

REGIONAL ECONOMIC
EXPANSION

ENERGY, MINES &
RESOURCES

NATIONAL REVENUE

JUSTICE

INDIAN AFFAIRS &
NORTHERN DEVELOPMENT

LABOUR

PRES. PRIVY COUNCIL

HEALTH & WELFARE

SECRETARY OF STATE

FISHERIES & FORESTRY

AGRICULTURE

VETERANS AFFAIRS

CONSUMER & CORPORATE
AFFAIRS

TRANSPORT

POSTMASTER-GENERAL

COMMUNICATIONS

SUPPLY & SERVICES

ENVIRONMENT

PARLIAMENT

HOUSE OF COMMONS

GOVERNMENT

OPPOSITION

SENATE
Most senators belong to one
of the major political parties

THE ELECTORATE

part of the unwritten constitution confirmed to the new Dominion by the provision that it should have "a constitution similar in principle to that of the United Kingdom." The House of Commons and the Senate, the latter the Canadian counterpart of the British House of Lords, complete the structure.

This, in brief outline, is the form of parliamentary government provided for in the British North America Act. We must now examine each section of the system in detail to see how it fits into the general scheme, what functions it performs and whether it might perform them better.

The Governor-General

When the Queen is in Canada, she is the head of the government, but in her absence she is represented by the Governor-General. After reading Sections 9-11 of the British North America Act, one might conclude that the Governor-General, assisted from time to time by the Privy Council, was really the government of Canada. We know, however, that this is not true any more than it is true that the Queen really governs the United Kingdom. Today both the Queen and her representative are symbols of the past in the sense that their positions are largely formal and possess honour and dignity but very little power. Such was not always the case, and much of Canada's constitutional history can be written in terms of changes in the powers of the Governor-General.

At one time the Governor of a British North American colony was indeed its governor. Although he was responsible to his superiors in London, his word was virtually law in the colony. But in 1759 in Nova Scotia, and by the Constitutional Act of 1791 in what are now Ontario and Quebec, the colonies were given elected assemblies, or representative governments. Outwardly, the appearance of government then was much the same as it is today. At the top was the Crown, in the person of the Governor. Advising the Governor was an Executive Council which he appointed. The Governor and his Council made up the executive branch of the government and corresponded to the Queen and Cabinet in Britain. The legislative or law-

REPRESENTATIVE AND RESPONSIBLE GOVERNMENT

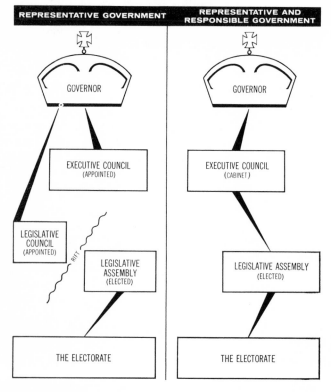

This chart highlights the differences between the system of representative government which characterized the British North American colonies until the late 1840's and the present system of responsible representative government. On the left the elected representatives of the people had no connection with, or control over, the executive branch of the government (Executive Council and Governor). Under the system of responsible government the people's elected representatives control the executive branch of government.

making branch consisted of an appointed Legislative Council and a Legislative Assembly elected by those people who had sufficient property to qualify as voters. These bodies, the Legislative Council and the Assembly, corresponded roughly to the House of Lords and House of Commons in Britain.

While the government was similar to that of today in outward appearance, in practice there was one great difference. Today the elected Assembly or House of Commons can control the executive, and has the final say in government. Formerly, the Governor and Executive Council were the most powerful branch of government. They could, and often did, act without the approval of the Assembly. The Assembly might pass bills but the Governor could refuse to accept them. Though the elected Assembly controlled taxation, the Governor and his Council usually had access to enough money from other sources (from customs duties, for example) to carry on the government, if need be, without the Assembly's co-operation.

This situation understandably led to constant wrangling between the Assembly on the one hand and the Governor and the Executive Council on the other. Eventually the bitterness flared into armed conflict in the famous Rebellions of 1837 led by Louis Joseph Papineau in Lower Canada and William Lyon Mackenzie in Upper Canada. Papineau and Mackenzie failed in their immediate objective of overthrowing the government, but the rebellions did convince the British government that all was not well in Canada, something that countless letters, petitions and memoranda had failed to do. John Lambton, first Earl of Durham, was sent from Britain to investigate the situation and suggest a solution. Durham's report on the colonies became one of the outstanding documents in the history of Britain, Canada and the Empire.

Durham believed in representative government; moreover, he was convinced that the wishes of the people, expressed by their elected representatives, should constitute the policy of the government. Yet in Canada the appointed members of the Executive Council dominated the government. Durham's solution was simple, and owed a good deal to the advice of Robert Baldwin, one of the leaders of the reform movement in Upper Canada. The Governor should choose his advisers from among those elected representatives who had the confidence of the Assembly and should follow their advice, instead of relying on the wealthy landowners, merchants and officials who had previously made up the appointed Executive Council. To stay in office as his advisers, these men would have to give the Governor such advice as the Assembly would support, for they would be *responsible* to the Assembly for their actions. If the Assembly ceased to approve their policies, the Governor would replace his advisers with men who did have the confidence of the Assembly. Representative government would thus become *responsible* government as well, since the Executive would be responsible to the Assembly, which in turn was responsible to the people. The differences between the two systems are set forth in chart form on page 50.

Although Durham's argument was widely applauded in Canada, where it had been most eloquently expressed by Robert Baldwin, it was not accepted in England. However, the Canadians, led by Baldwin and Louis Lafontaine, persisted in advocating it and eventually the British agreed to put it into practice. Responsible government came into effect in 1846 in Nova Scotia under Sir John Harvey, and in 1848-49 in Canada under Lord Elgin. It was confirmed in Canada in 1849 when Lord Elgin signed the Rebellion Losses Bill, although he did not approve of it.

The Growth of Self-Government

The achievement of responsible government by the British North American colonies did not mean that they were fully self-governing. Britain still exercised wide powers over them. The young colonies had no voice at all in external affairs. And though Britain's aim was to interfere as little as possible in internal colonial matters, there was in fact no doubt that she had the power to do so if she wished.

The Governor, as the instrument by which the British government supervised and controlled the colonies, had extensive powers. He made certain that all laws passed by

STAGES IN THE GROWTH OF AUTONOMY

1846: Governor instructed to introduce responsible government

1849: Lord Elgin's signing the Rebellion Losses Bill confirmed responsible government in Canada.

1858: Galt's Tariff established Canada's independence in economic affairs.

1867: Confederation—the beginning of a nation

1871: Withdrawal of Imperial troops from Canada

1880: Appointment of a Canadian High Commissioner to Britain

1887-1911: Imperial and Colonial Conferences

1904: A Canadian commander appointed for the Canadian militia

1909: Creation of the Department of External Affairs

1914: Canada determined the extent of her participation in the First World War.

1917: The Canadian Corps placed under the command of Sir Arthur Currie, a Canadian
Imperial Conference on the nature of the post-war Empire
Formation of the Imperial War Cabinet with Dominion Prime Ministers as members

1919: Canada asserted its right to sign peace treaties. Canada became a member of the League of Nations.

1922: The Chanak crisis determined Canada's right to be consulted in British foreign policy proposed for the Empire.

1923: At the Imperial Conference Canada successfully asserted its right to have its own foreign policy.
The Halibut Treaty with the United States, the first treaty signed between Canada and a foreign nation

1925: Canada is not bound by British agreements in Locarno treaties

1926: The Balfour Report to the Imperial Conference gave a definition of the modern Commonwealth.

1931: The Statute of Westminster removed all signs of colonial subordination.

1939: Canada declared war on Germany independently of Britain.

1949: Appeals to the Privy Council abolished

19—: Passage of B.N.A. Act by Canadian Parliament and constitutional amendment in Canada the Colonial Assemblies were sent to England for approval, where they might be disallowed by the British government. He could prevent bills from becoming law by reserving them for the consideration of the British government. All correspondence between Britain and the colony had to pass through his hands. Thus, even with the achievement of responsible government, the Governor still had a great deal of power. Though he had to accept the advice of his ministers in regard to internal matters, he could control anything which involved imperial affairs or the mother country. As long as Britain had any effective control over Canada, that is, as long as Canada remained a colony, the Governor-General was bound to be an important figure.

The story of Canada's development from colony to nation is a long and dramatic one. Various stages in the growth of Canadian autonomy are shown on page 53. The most important event was the 1926 Imperial Conference where it was recognized that the self-governing colonies known as Dominions were "equal in status" and "in no way subordinate" to the mother country. Britain was no longer to exercise any authority over them. The Governor-General then ceased to be an imperial officer representing the British government, and became simply the representative of the monarch. Choice of a man to fill the post rested with the government of Canada. At present the Governor-General, the personal representative of Elizabeth II, Queen of Canada, is His Excellency Roland Michener, who is a citizen of Canada.

Today responsible government is the essence of our parliamentary system. It means simply that the Governor will act in most instances on the advice of his ministers. His acts are merely the formal method of putting into effect whatever policy his ministers plan. These ministers, or the Cabinet as they are collectively called, are in turn responsible to the House of Commons and can hold office as advisers to the Crown only as long as they are supported by the elected House. If they are defeated in an election or in the House of Commons, they must resign. Under the present system of responsible government the Governor's role is largely a formal one; real executive power is exercised by the Prime Minister and the other ministers in the Cabinet.

Powers of the Governor-General

Is it true then, as some people have argued, that the Governor-General is now only a figurehead, a rubber stamp for the Cabinet? Could we not do without this office in the government? To answer these questions we must examine what rights, powers and influence the Governor-General has.

The primary duty of the Governor-General is to see that the government of the country is carried on. If the Prime Minister died tomorrow, the Governor-General would have to find a replacement for him. True, he would probably wait until the ministers or prominent party members had met and selected a new leader, or, if Parliament were in session, until a caucus or meeting of the Members of Parliament of the government party had chosen a successor. If Parliament were not in session, however, or if the party members could not quickly agree on a leader, the Governor-General would have to select personally a new Prime Minister and ask him to form a government. The choice of the Governor-General would be limited, however, for the new leader would have to be supported in Parliament.

The occasion of Sir John Thompson's sudden death in London in 1894 affords one illustration of the Governor-General's task in selecting a new Prime Minister. Lady Aberdeen, wife of the Governor-General, summarized the problem in her diary:

> It is a delicate position. This has come so suddenly that there has been no preparing for any successor and Mr. Mackenzie Bowell was only appointed acting premier in Sir John's absence quite in a temporary way. Mr. Foster, the Minister of Finance, is an able man, a good speaker & a good man, but he has no power over other men & showed no power for leading in the House once before when Sir John was away. And then that clique against him & his wife, because they married in the United States after she had divorced her husband, makes a difficulty. And Mr. Haggart who is the strongest man is admittedly a Bohemian & also ill—he would

probably not serve under Mr. Foster nor Mr. Foster
under him. Mr. Mackenzie Bowell himself is 75, rather
fussy & decidedly commonplace, also an Orangeman, at
one time the Grand Master of the Orangemen of North
America & also past president of the tip-top Grand
Orange affairs at Belfast—but he is a good & straight
man & has great ideas about the drawing together of
the colonies & the Empire, as was evidenced by all the
trouble he took about getting up that Conference. But
there is no one to consult & we have but little indication of Sir John's feelings.

In the end Lord Aberdeen asked Mackenzie Bowell to
form a new government, and after much bickering and
muted threats of revolt the other members of Thompson's
Cabinet accepted the Governor-General's decision.

Today, with our multi-party system and minority governments, a situation might arise in which the Governor-
General would have to play a role in the selection of a
government. Parties could be so evenly matched after an
election that several leaders might claim the Prime Minis-
tership. Even the leader of a small party might have the
best chance of forming a coalition government. In such
cases the Governor-General might have to exercise his dis-
cretion.

Many authorities contend that the Governor-General
has a duty to ensure that the government does not use its
powers unfairly. If the Prime Minister requests a dissolution of Parliament and a new election, it is the duty of the
Governor-General to make sure that the request is a reasonable one. In 1926 Lord Byng, then Governor-General
of Canada, concluded that Mackenzie King's request for a
dissolution was not reasonable and refused it. King there-
upon resigned, but later won the election of that year.
After the 1965 election, which returned Mr. Pearson to
office without a majority, Mr. Diefenbaker argued that if
Mr. Pearson were defeated in the Commons the Governor-
General should not give him another dissolution but instead
should invite the Conservative leader to try to form a government.

Some people also hold the view that the Governor-

This cartoon, labelled "Advice to the little partisan politician—DON'T," appeared during the famous King-Byng crisis in 1926. The election of 1925 had returned more Conservatives than Liberals, but King felt that he could carry on and maintain a majority with the support of the Progressive Party. But when a scandal was revealed, the Progressives no longer supported King and he was defeated. King then asked for a dissolution and another election, but Lord Byng—quite properly, most authorities argue—replied that since Meighen actually had the largest party he should have the opportunity to see if he could form a government.

Despite the warning issued by the cartoon, King made a political issue out of the affair, claiming that the refusal of a British official to follow the advice of his Canadian Prime Minister was an indication of colonial status for Canada.

General should make sure that his ministers obey the law. He should see that charges of wrong-doing against the government are properly and fairly examined. He can, if need be, dismiss a government that has been guilty of corruption. Lord Dufferin was prepared to dismiss Sir John A. Macdonald in 1873 over the Pacific Scandal, but Macdonald resigned when he realized he could not continue in office in the face of public criticism.

These political powers of the Governor-General, however, are not very important. The problem of choosing a new Prime Minister, other than after an election, will rarely occur, and it can be solved in other ways than by action of the Governor-General. Seldom, it is hoped, will a government become so scandalously corrupt and so immune to public opinion that its dismissal would be necessary. If this were all the Crown's representative did, we might well question the wisdom of retaining the office.

But he performs other duties. The Governor-General's chief function in practice is to be the dignified social and ceremonial head of the government. He is the person the public sees, the distinguished layer of cornerstones, opener of hospitals, greeter of foreign dignitaries, patron of good causes and events. Viscount Alexander, the last British Governor-General, is said to have spent considerable time practising for the ceremonial kick-off of a Grey Cup football game. Our society seems to demand all of this, and a uniformed and ribboned Governor-General makes an imposing figure at such ceremonies. The Prime Minister and his Cabinet are thus left free to concentrate on their executive duties, unhampered by the need for ceremonial appearances, unless they wish to make them (as they often do for political purposes).

More important, probably, is the fact that the Governor-General represents or symbolizes the history of our system of government. When the Queen opened the Canadian Parliament in October 1957, Canadian television viewers witnessed a ceremony that in essentials transported them back to the Middle Ages. The opening of every session of Parliament—the arrival of the Governor-General's carriage before the main entrance to the Parliament Buildings, the stately procession to the Senate Chamber, the invitation through Black Rod to the Commons to attend at the Bar of the Senate, and the Speech from the Throne—speaks volumes of history. (See pages 68-9.)

One cannot measure the value of such formal occasions. They are a reminder that what is did not always exist. They bring to an old lumber town on the Ottawa River the majesty and drama of a thousand years of struggle for free institutions.

The Cabinet

The real executive in Canada is not the Crown but the Cabinet. This is where the great difference lies between the appearance and the reality of the parliamentary system. The Cabinet has been variously described as "the core of the British constitutional system," "the centre of gravity" where "the whole weight of government is in a very real sense concentrated," the machine of state and the nerve centre of the government. So important is the Cabinet that many people use the words *Cabinet* and *government* as though they were synonymous.

Simply stated, the Cabinet is composed of the Prime Minister and anyone else he chooses. Almost always he selects members of his party who have seats in Parliament, usually in the House of Commons. The Cabinet is therefore composed of the leading members of the dominant political party.

Sometimes, because of special qualifications, distinguished non-members of Parliament are invited to join the Cabinet, as was Dr. Sidney Smith, President of the University of Toronto, in 1957. Such a person is required by "invariable custom" to acquire a seat as soon as possible, and the government may either appoint him to the Senate or persuade a Member for a "safe" constituency to resign and thus open a seat in the Commons. The government found a "safe" seat for Dr. Smith, but in 1945 General McNaughton was less fortunate. In November 1944, Prime Minister King had appointed him to the Cabinet as Minister of National Defence in an attempt to stimulate recruiting. In February 1945, the supposedly "safe" riding of

"Thanks for coming, fellows — I'll see you all at the same time tomorrow."

Talkative cabinet ministers have always been the favourites of reporters, who are desperate to file copy on the real or imagined
decisions of the Cabinet. As soon as Mr. Trudeau took office he
attempted to stop the leaks that had often embarrassed the Pearson
government.

Grey North elected a Conservative instead of the General.
As a result he left the Cabinet a few months later.

The men the Prime Minister chooses are sworn in as
Privy Councillors by the Governor-General and become
the active part of the Privy Council, or the Cabinet. Before
examining the reasons for the Prime Minister's choice of
his cabinet ministers, let us first see what the Cabinet does.

The Cabinet as a whole, composed of leading members
of the winning political party, determines government policy. Although it must secure parliamentary approval, the
Cabinet makes the initial decision whether the country will
be at peace or at war, whether taxes will be raised or
lowered, whether an airport will be built here or a post
office there. In short, every government action either originates in, or has been approved by, the Cabinet. The Cabinet *is* in many ways the government.

Each member of the Cabinet is normally in charge of a
government department—Agriculture, National Defence,
Public Works, Finance, Justice and others. Each minister
presents his department's needs and wishes before the

Cabinet, where decisions are reached after examination and discussion. Broader matters involving the national welfare are brought before the Cabinet by the Prime Minister or by an interested member of the Cabinet, and general agreement on these issues is reached.

As the functions of government change, so too does the nature of the Cabinet. There is a continual change in the titles of the cabinet ministers, as the government regroups their tasks. Early in 1971 Parliament approved a bill which gave the government power to create Ministers of State, or cabinet ministers, for specially designated purposes. The first new department to be created was a Department of Environment, and as this book is going to press Departments of Urban Affairs and of Science Policy are in the planning stages. In addition to cabinet ministers with specific responsibilities, there are also Ministers without Portfolio who take on whatever assignments may be given to them by the Prime Minister. Finally, the Cabinet also includes the government leader in the Senate.

A Cabinet of thirty members is an unwieldly group. With his passion for efficiency, Prime Minister Trudeau reorganized the operation of the Cabinet soon after he took office in 1968. He scrapped the fourteen cabinet committees that had existed under Mr. Pearson, and established four new and more powerful committees: external policy and defence; economic policy; communications, works and urban affairs; and social policy, including manpower and labour. Each of these committees was to be a miniature Cabinet, with the power to make final decisions. These decisions were, however, subject to review by the full Cabinet. In addition, four coordinating committees were established. The senior committee on priorities and planning was like an inner Cabinet, and was to plan long-term government strategy and issue guidelines for other cabinet committees. The others dealt with legislation, government spending, and federal-provincial relations.

Each cabinet minister is responsible for the operation of his department. In Parliament he must explain the activities and policies of his department, and answer whatever questions the Opposition asks. He knows, however, that

his colleagues in the Cabinet are behind him, for an attack
on one is an attack on all. If a measure involving one
department is defeated in the Commons, the entire Cabinet
must resign.

Collective Responsibility

This practice is known as the principle of collective
responsibility. In the secret cabinet meetings the members
may disagree as much as they like, but once a decision is
reached members of the Cabinet must support it or resign.
Sometimes, when it is known that a certain minister is
really opposed to a particular policy adopted by his colleagues, the newspapers and opposition members will bait
and harass him in the hope that he will speak out and
embarrass his fellow ministers. This strategy seldom works.
Sometimes, however, we see the strange spectacle of two

OTTAWA ARMAMENT WORKS

cabinet ministers unwittingly contradicting each other. Such a situation embarrasses the Prime Minister (who will soon have them on the carpet) while it delights and, perhaps, aids the Opposition. Before the downfall of Mr. Diefenbaker's government in 1963 the country was treated to the spectacle of the Minister of Defence, Mr. Harkness, and the Secretary of State for External Affairs, Mr. Green, disagreeing publicly over Canadian policy with respect to nuclear weapons. Ultimately, being unable to agree with the Party, Mr. Harkness resigned and was later followed by two other members of the Cabinet.

The same fissures have been seen in Mr. Trudeau's Cabinet. In April 1969 Paul Hellyer, the leading opponent of Mr. Trudeau at the Liberal leadership convention in 1968, suddenly resigned his seat in the Cabinet. The issue, said Mr. Hellyer, was that he could not accept the Prime Minister's view that since housing fell largely within provincial jurisdiction the federal government was incapable of effective action to solve Canada's housing shortage. In April 1971 Eric Kierans followed Paul Hellyer into the political wilderness. For some time Mr. Kierans had opposed the economic policies of the government in the cabinet discussions. Unable to persuade the Prime Minister and his colleagues to adopt his view of economic policy, he resigned. As he wrote to Mr. Trudeau: "To challenge openly long-established policies and practices would be embarrassing to my colleagues and to you, and unfair, if I were to remain in the Cabinet."

The resignations of powerful political figures reveal one of the striking features of the Canadian Cabinet—the dominance of the Prime Minister. As Mr. Hellyer said, "there is no way the Cabinet can buck the Prime Minister." A strong Prime Minister makes his authority felt in the Cabinet. Major appointments and major decisions always reflect his views. There are two main reasons for the Prime Minister's paramount position. If it is true, as we have suggested, that most people vote for the party leader rather than for an individual candidate or a party, then both his colleagues and his party are indebted to him. Furthermore, since he can choose his cabinet colleagues at will, he can

remove them at will also. Every minister knows that there
are many other Members of Parliament eager to hold his
position. Rarely in Canadian history have there been
cabinet ministers strong enough politically to challenge
seriously the Prime Minister, and in almost every case their
challenges were unsuccessful. Only in 1896 was a revolt in
the Cabinet able to force the resignation of the Prime
Minister and in that instance there were seven strong
ministers and one very old and weak Prime Minister.

Cabinet Building

In selecting his Cabinet the Prime Minister has a difficult
task, for not only is the Cabinet made up of heads of
government departments but, far more important, it must
take in all leading members of the party in power. The
Prime Minister tries to choose men who combine administrative talent with political influence. Unfortunately for the
nation, administrative ability and political influence are not
always combined in the same individual. Moreover, the
Prime Minister must not only reward the "strong men" of
the party; he must also try to keep all sections of the party
pleased. In a vast country like Canada, where the interests
of its many regions are different, and sometimes even
opposed, this is no easy task.

   Certain customs governing the selection of cabinet members have become firmly fixed. For instance it is the custom to appoint at least one Member of Parliament from
each province to a cabinet post, although tiny Prince Edward Island, with fewer voters than York-Scarborough and
only as many seats as Winnipeg, has sometimes been disappointed. Neither Saskatchewan nor Alberta elected any
Liberals to the House of Commons in 1965, and the two
provinces remained without any representatives in the Cabinet. Quebec has always expected to have at least four of
its representatives in the Cabinet, three French-speaking
and one English-speaking, and Ontario has demanded one
more than Quebec. These members have increased as the
Cabinet has grown, and today it appears that six each
from Ontario and Quebec may be the accepted minimum.
Prime Minister St. Laurent had six from each; Prime

Minister Diefenbaker had six from Ontario and five from Quebec for the session of 1960, but promised to fill "Quebec's other seat." In 1963 Mr. Pearson appointed ten from Ontario—including himself and one senator—and eight from Quebec. Mr. Trudeau, suffering a shortage of Members from the west and the Maritimes, has ten from each of Ontario and Quebec, one from each of Alberta, Saskatchewan, Nova Scotia, New Brunswick and Newfoundland and three from British Columbia (June 1971).

To increase the Prime Minister's difficulties, different religious and racial groups within Canada feel that they should be represented in the Cabinet. Naturally few Prime Ministers willingly annoy any substantial section of the electorate. The result of this recognition of party stalwarts, leaders of factions, and provincial, religious and racial claims is that the Cabinet may not always represent the best talents in the party. Alexander Mackenzie, the Liberal Prime Minister from 1873 to 1878, once complained bitterly about his Cabinet that "my real trouble has been the results of sectional representation forcing upon me men of so inferior calibre as to be utterly useless as assistants. . . ." On another occasion he wrote of the Cabinet which party needs and sectional interests had forced on him in less than affectionate terms: "Mr. B. won't take a hand unless everything is as clear as day. . . . Huntingdon is willing but he is not industrious. . . . Smith is lazy. Burpee knows his own business nothing more. Vail I cannot let loose. Coffin has neither talent tongue or sense [sic]. . . . Cauchon no use. Scott . . . often blunders in the Senate. . . ."

To summarize: the Cabinet is the real executive. It is led by the Prime Minister and is composed of members of his party who usually have won seats in the House of Commons. It determines and initiates government policy. Almost every member is individually responsible for the supervision of a department of government. Collectively they are responsible to the House of Commons and the people for their decisions. The Cabinet comes before the people in an election every four or five years to account for its actions. In the meantime, it is watched by the House of Commons where it must present its measures every year.

The Legislature

Government or cabinet decisions can be put into effect in two ways. On many minor matters the Governor-General is simply advised by the Cabinet to consent to a measure which then becomes law as an Order in Council, that is, an order passed by the Governor-General in Council. (The fiction is still maintained that the Governor-

THE PASSAGE OF A BILL

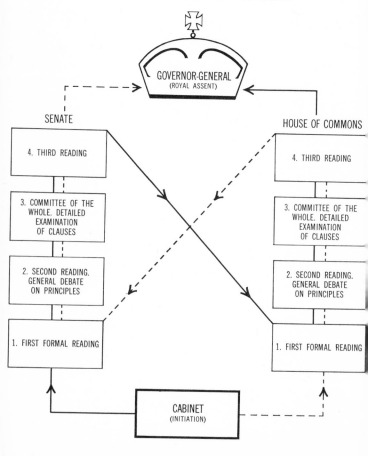

GOVERNOR-GENERAL
(ROYAL ASSENT)

SENATE

4. THIRD READING

3. COMMITTEE OF THE WHOLE. DETAILED EXAMINATION OF CLAUSES

2. SECOND READING. GENERAL DEBATE ON PRINCIPLES

1. FIRST FORMAL READING

HOUSE OF COMMONS

4. THIRD READING

3. COMMITTEE OF THE WHOLE. DETAILED EXAMINATION OF CLAUSES

2. SECOND READING. GENERAL DEBATE ON PRINCIPLES

1. FIRST FORMAL READING

CABINET
(INITIATION)

General does attend Council meetings, although this is no longer the case. Nor does the whole Council meet but only that committee of it which is the Cabinet.) Major policies, however, have to be put into effect by Acts passed by Parliament. Bills are drawn up by various ministers (in fact by the civil servants, following the general lines laid down by the ministers) and presented to the House of Commons and the Senate. Since the Cabinet is composed of leading members of the majority party, it is highly unlikely that a bill coming from the Cabinet will fail to pass. Thus, in addition to its executive function, the Cabinet is also responsible for the great bulk of legislation.

The legislature in any governmental system is the body of persons which has the power to make, alter or repeal the laws of the country. There are two chambers or houses in the Canadian legislature, the House of Commons and the Senate. Both houses must hold yearly sessions. As the chart opposite indicates, any bill must be passed by a majority in both chambers before it can be placed before the Governor-General for his assent and become a law. Money bills must originate in the House of Commons but bills on other subjects may be introduced in either house. Apart from this apparent equality, however, the chambers have little in common. The House of Commons is regarded as the very citadel of representative and democratic government. The Senate is often looked upon with amusement and even contempt, and the argument is commonly heard that it should be reformed or abolished completely. We must examine the validity of both these views.

The House of Commons

The House of Commons is the representative body in the parliamentary system. We have seen how Members of the Canadian House of Commons are elected, how the selection of the Prime Minister and Cabinet depends upon the party standings in the Commons, and how the Cabinet is responsible to the House of Commons and must always be able to command a majority there. Every bill must be passed by the Commons as an essential step to its becoming a law or statute. In practice, all important government measures are introduced in the House, although any can be

THE OPENING

The Parliament of Canada is usually opened by the
Governor-General who represents the Queen. (But if
the Queen is in Canada she will open Parliament
herself, as she did in 1957.)

Before entering the Parliament Buildings, the
Governor-General reviews an honour guard. Then,
preceded by the Gentleman Usher of the Black Rod,
he moves to the Senate Chamber and takes his seat
on the Throne. The presence at the annual opening
of Parliament of the judges of the Supreme Court of
Canada reminds us of the judicial origins of the
High Court of Parliament which is the supreme law-
making authority in the land.

When the Governor-General has been seated,
Black Rod goes to House of Commons to ask the
Members and the Speaker to come to Senate to hear
the Speech from the Throne. Ever since Charles I
entered the House to arrest some of its Members, the
Commons has always been vigilant to maintain its
independence, and the King has never been allowed
inside its doors. Although no such fears exist today,
Black Rod's journey to the Commons reminds us of
the early history of Parliament. As he approaches,
the door of the House of Commons is slammed in
his face. His three knocks with his ebony staff bring
the question from inside, "Who is there?" Upon
replying, "Black Rod," he is admitted and advances
a few steps inside the House. Bowing three times to
the Speaker, he informs the Commons of the Governor-General's command to go to the Senate.

Black Rod then moves slowly and ceremoniously
out of the House of Commons. Preceded by the

OF PARLIAMENT

Speaker, the Members of the House follow him. The Sergeant-at-Arms carries the Mace, originally a weapon of defence, but now the symbol of the authority of the House of Commons.

When the Members of the House of Commons reach the Senate they stand outside the bar of the Chamber to listen to the Speech from the Throne. The Speech was originally an expression of the monarch's wishes. Now, although its wording may sound the same, the Governor-General reads a statement prepared by the Prime Minister announcing the programme which the government will place before Parliament during the session.

Seated to the Governor-General's right during the reading of the Speech is the Prime Minister. Although a Member of the Commons, he is permitted to enter the Senate because of his position as the Governor-General's chief adviser or Privy Councillor.

When the Speech from the Throne has been read, the Members of the House of Commons return to their Chamber. The Mace is placed in its position on the table to signify that the House is officially in session. Although generally directed in the Speech to attend to matters mentioned in it, the Commons, again to show its independence, introduces briefly a subject of its own choosing. This formality over, the House, showing that it represents the people of Canada, begins its consideration of the Speech from the Throne. In session, the House of Commons is presided over by the Speaker, who is usually elected from the majority party. The government party sits to his right, and the Opposition to his left.

introduced in the Senate, and some are. (See page 66.) By custom all cabinet ministers heading departments must either hold seats in the Commons or seek early election to the Commons. (When Mr. Diefenbaker appointed Wallace McCutcheon to the Senate in 1962 and gave him an important position in the Cabinet there was considerable criticism because Mr. McCutcheon could not answer in the House which represented the people.)

NOT A VINTAGE YEAR

Backbenchers are not always content with their role. In recent years they have insisted on more information, more consultation, and more power in influencing government decisions. In 1969 backbenchers such as Phil Givens, once Mayor of Toronto, (pictured here as the waiter) proved to be a troublesome and hardheaded crew for the Trudeau Cabinet.

The House of Commons is, therefore, the supreme body in the parliamentary system. The Cabinet would seem to be less important, for once it ceases to have the support of the House of Commons it must resign. The House can indicate its displeasure by defeating a government measure or simply by passing a motion of lack of confidence in the ministers. In such cases, the Prime Minister has no alternative but to hand in his resignation to the Governor-General or ask for a dissolution. It would seem then that the Prime Minister and his cabinet colleagues should live in daily dread of the House of Commons, watching fearfully for signs that their masters in the Commons were losing confidence in them.

Such is seldom the case. In fact, for years Canadians complained that the Cabinet treated the House of Commons with contempt rather than fearful respect. There are several reasons for the apparently dominant position of the Cabinet. For one thing, it is the Prime Minister and Cabinet, not the private Member from Beaver Creek, who are the leaders of the party. Many Members realize that they owe their seats to the appeal of the Prime Minister or to the strength and popularity of the Cabinet. Furthermore, both the Cabinet and the majority in the Commons belong to the same political party, and many Members believe that party unity is necessary above all else. In addition party organizers outside Parliament and men known as party whips in the Commons constantly remind them of the need for solidarity. In other words, the Cabinet usually has a majority in the Commons who, in most circumstances, will vote as they are told. In the private party meetings, known as the caucus, backbenchers can complain about government policy, but, as with the Cabinet, once the majority decision has been taken they present a solid front to the Opposition. In every Parliament there are rebels, but they soon learn that in rebelling they are ruining their chances of advancement in the party and will likely remain humble backbenchers gazing in envy, if not in admiration, on the cabinet ministers in the front benches.

In short, the Cabinet needs only to be really concerned about defeat in the House of Commons if party discipline is so weak that the authority of the leaders is challenged, or if the party has only a slight majority of the seats, or if, as after the 1962, 1963 and 1965 elections, it has a minority of the seats. Such cases have been very rare in Canadian history. The dominance of the Prime Minister and Cabinet over the majority in the Commons has been so constant that some people have suggested that the House, like the Governor-General, is little more than a rubber stamp.

Role of the Opposition

While it is true that the Cabinet usually has its way in the Commons, the Opposition is there to put forward constructive criticism. The leader of the Opposition, usually the head of the second-largest party in the House, is paid by the state (in addition to his pay as a Member of Parliament) to lead the criticism of the government. He is an alternative Prime Minister and must be prepared to take over the reins of government if his party should defeat the government in the House or in an election.

Although the government controls the business of the House, opposition members from other parties are ensured an opportunity to voice their opinions. Debates are conducted according to established rules under the impartial chairmanship of the Speaker. There are also question periods during which any Member may question the ministers and demand, even if he does not always get, a full answer. In the major debates and question periods, the operation of government can be subjected to a close scrutiny. However, much of the most valuable work is done in small committees where the activities of various departments are closely examined or the details of bills hammered out.

Probably the chief value of the meetings of the Commons is to keep the activities of the government in open view. The government must explain and justify its policies in front of the Opposition and the Press Gallery and thus, through newspaper, radio and television reports, in front of the people. The parties in opposition suggest weaknesses in these policies and put forward their own proposals. If there are skeletons in the government's closet, the Opposition will attempt to drag them out into the daylight. In November 1964, for example, an Opposition M.P. unearthed the Rivard scandal, charging that political influence had been used to attempt to prevent Lucien Rivard from being extradited to the United States. The three opposition parties then forced a reluctant government to appoint the Dorion inquiry to investigate the case.

It is the Opposition, then, that is really the people's watchdog between elections. Sometimes, however, the opposition spokesmen oppose or criticize to no good purpose and become obstructive. Often the Opposition does not have enough material at its disposal to examine the government's actions adequately, and the government is understandably reluctant to give out information that might be politically damaging to it. Alarmed by what appears to be an ever-widening gap between the people and their government, the Toronto *Globe and Mail*, in a front-page editorial on June 4, 1960, wrote:

> . . . cabinet ministers refuse essential information to the parliamentary bodies which in theory govern, but without such information cannot govern; which in theory are supreme, but without such information are no more than rubber stamps. Public men, so called, are increasingly unavailable to the public. They conceal themselves behind anonymous spokesmen, press officers, public relations advisers and the like. The ordinary citizen asks in vain for an accounting of what is being done with his money, what is happening to his country.

On both government and opposition benches, too much time is taken up in reading long-winded speeches directed mainly at the voters back home, deploring the high cost of tractors (if the speaker represents a farming community) or applauding the decision to raise the import duty on shoe laces (if there happens to be a shoe-lace factory in the speaker's constituency) . The House, like the Cabinet, has its share of dead wood. Each session points up the fact that a good campaigner is not necessarily a good parliamentarian. Some Members have not made a speech in the

"Filibuster? Who, me?"

Sometimes the Opposition's determination to slow down or prevent legislation from passing the Commons moves beyond the bounds of legitimate enquiry and criticism to deliberate obstruction, called filibustering. A case of this was provided by the famous flag debate in 1964 when the Conservatives, led by Mr. Diefenbaker, sought to prevent the adoption of the new Canadian flag.

If the opposition members clearly reveal that they plan to obstruct urgent government legislation, the government can introduce closure. This device, first used in 1913, curtails discussion and forces an early vote. Closure has seldom been used, however, because it is more dangerous than it is effective. In 1956, for example, when the Conservatives, led by George Drew, made it clear that they planned to obstruct the pipeline bill, the St. Laurent government, at the urging of Mr. Howe, applied closure. The outcry in the House of Commons and throughout the country that the Liberals were destroying the rights of free speech and of Parliament caused the matter to become one of the chief issues in the 1957 election which brought about the Liberal downfall after twenty-two years in office.

House for twenty-five years; others would have done the country more good by remaining silent more often. Yet many men who make poor debaters do valuable work in the parliamentary committees.

The Senate

The second chamber in the legislature is the Senate. It is not an elected body like the House of Commons, but is composed of one hundred and two men appointed by the Governor-General on the advice of his ministers. In effect this means appointed by the Prime Minister who will, of course, consult his colleagues in most cases. To be a Senator, one must be at least thirty years of age and have property to the value of not less than $4,000. Once appointed, a Senator used to remain in office for life unless he was declared bankrupt, committed an infamous crime or failed to attend two consecutive sessions. In 1965, however, the Pearson government passed a law making retirement compulsory at 75 for all future Senators.

The Senate's chief task is to consider legislation. In theory its functions differ little from those of the House of Commons. With the exception of money bills, any legislation may be introduced first in the Senate if the Cabinet wishes. On the surface, then, the two chambers seem to be equally important.

Most Canadians know that the Senate is by no means equal to the House of Commons. Many, in fact, argue that it has no value at all. In the first place, the doctrine of responsible government has to do with the relation of the Cabinet to the Commons. Defeated in the Commons, a government must resign; defeated in the Senate, it goes right along as though nothing had happened. So unconcerned is the government about what goes on in the Senate that as a rule only one cabinet minister sits there, and this only because someone has to be responsible for conducting government business in the Senate. The cabinet minister in the Senate does not usually head a department of government and is known as Leader of the Government in the Senate. Debates are not an important part of the Senate's activities and they are seldom reported in the press. The debates of the Senate fill only one volume a year, whereas those of the Commons fill seven or eight huge ones. Since the Senators do not represent the people directly, their views, no matter how intelligent and accurate, seldom receive as much consideration as those of Members of the House. Moreover, since the Senators are usually party appointees and, up until recently, were appointed for life, the majority of them are likely to belong to whichever party has held office most in the preceding twenty years or so, but not necessarily to the party currently in power. In 1959, after twenty-five years of Liberal reign, there were seventy-three Senators with Liberal affiliations and only eighteen Conservatives.

In view of all this we may well ask two questions: Why do we have a Senate? And should we have a Senate at all? By answering the first question we shall go a long way towards answering the second.

Functions of the Senate

The Canadian Senate embodies two functions: that of an upper chamber, which is traditional in the British type of constitution, and that of protector of provincial rights in a federal system. When the British granted representative institutions to the colonies, they attempted to duplicate in broad outline the British constitution, which included the original upper chamber, the House of Lords. It was not just a blind following of tradition, for it was felt that appointed upper houses, composed of men of substance, would be a good check on the unrestrained will of the people and their elected Assemblies. At that time the colonies in British North America all had appointed upper houses called Legislative Councils. When the delegates from the colonies gathered to draft a constitution for the new Canada between 1864 and 1867, they readily agreed that the new country should also have an upper chamber. They called it the Senate.

As a check on the unrestrained will of the people the Senate has hardly been necessary. The Canadian people and their representatives in the Commons have normally moved so slowly that any further restraint has not been needed. Moreover, democratic beliefs have become so much more widely accepted in the past century that few Canadians would be prepared to let an appointed Senate stand in the way of an elected Commons. On the few occasions when the Senate has taken a firm stand against the wishes of the government and a majority in the Commons, a majority of the Senators have usually belonged to the Opposition. A Liberal Senate, for example, threw out a

FIREBUG

When in 1961 the Senate, dominated by the Liberals, threw out a Conservative tariff bill which permitted tariff increases without appeal to a board of review, Prime Minister Diefenbaker vaguely threatened to call an election. The issue would inevitably have been whether to end or mend the Senate. Cartoonist Duncan Macpherson pictured Mr. Diefenbaker as a Nero who would play an election reel while the Senate burned. The Prime Minister drew back, however, perhaps feeling that the people would support the Senate, or that the time was not ripe for a general election.

Conservative bill to supply money to Great Britain for the building of dreadnoughts in 1912. Had the Conservatives wished to press the matter they could have dissolved the House of Commons and consulted the wishes of the people in an election. If the Conservatives had won, the Senate would almost certainly have given way. Today it is doubtful that the Senate would reject a government bill, unless it felt that the people were opposed to it. In July 1960, however, it amended a bill dealing with the retirement of judges at seventy-five, and the Conservative government reluctantly accepted the amendment. In 1961 the Liberal Senate stubbornly refused to pass without amendment an important bill enabling the government to increase tariffs, and bluntly defied the Diefenbaker government when it tried to dismiss the Governor of the Bank of Canada on grounds which most Canadians, judging by the Gallup Poll and newspaper editorials, felt were inadequate.

It was never really intended that the Senate should compete with the House of Commons in legislation or, as Sir Robert Borden once said, "exercise its powers to the legal limit." Sir John A. Macdonald, Canada's first Prime Minister, and one of the architects of our constitution, had a different function in mind when he said in the 1865 debates on Confederation:

> It must be an independent House, having a free action of its own, for it is only valuable as being a regulating body, calmly considering the legislation initiated by the popular branch, and preventing any hasty or ill-considered legislation which may come from that body, but it will never set itself in opposition against the deliberate and understood wishes of the people.

Sir John was doubtless thinking of the Senate as a revising chamber, taking a "sober second look" at legislation, examining all its implications, perfecting the grammar of the text and so on. Since 1867 the Senate, especially through its committees, has done very useful work criticizing and amending bills. Seldom, however, has it changed their essential content. That this work of revision has become one of the main functions of the Senate was emphasized

not long ago when one of the most prominent Senators
said that the upper chamber was a judicial and not a
political institution. No one questions the value of this
work but some people have asked whether a hundred and
two men are needed to do it.

THE DRUDGE

When this cartoon appeared in 1960, divorce requests from Quebec
and Newfoundland were first presented and examined in the Senate
and then, if approved, were sent to the Commons for approval as a
bill. Hundreds of these bills would appear in the Commons and, as
had been the case for decades, they would be passed en masse without examination or comment. In 1960-61, two young C.C.F. Members
in the Commons determined to end what they regarded as a misuse
and mockery of Parliament, and particularly of the Commons. When
the bills arrived, they subjected them to searching examination,
effectively filibustering the work of the House. The same strategy was
followed in 1962. Soon they had fixed the public eye on the subject,
and in 1963-64 the government passed a bill providing for a judge to
act as the Senate divorce commissioner and enabling the Senate, by
simple resolution, to grant a divorce for which there was legally
acceptable grounds. In 1968 the Divorce Act made these two provinces
responsible for their own divorces.

In practice all private bills*, that is, bills relating only to individuals, corporations and so on, and not of public concern, originate in the Senate. Here they receive a detailed examination and the House of Commons is thus saved considerable time and trouble.

Yet in the eyes of its severer critics, none of these functions makes the Senate worthwhile. They argue that the provincial governments have functioned perfectly well without spending large sums to maintain an upper house. In any case they say that the Senate was primarily designed to represent minority and provincial interests, and its value should be determined by how well it performs that function.

As we know, Canada is a federation of former colonies. When these colonies agreed to unite to form the Dominion of Canada in 1867 many people were afraid that the colonies, which now became provinces, would be hopelessly submerged in the new nation. One safeguard against this was the creation of a Senate designed to act as the protector of provincial interests.

In the American federal system each state, regardless of its population, elects two Senators, and this has had the effect of making the Senate the bulwark of states' rights. In Canada, the Fathers of Confederation agreed on a scheme of regional representation. There were to be twenty-four Senators from Ontario, twenty-four from Quebec, and twenty-four from the Maritime provinces. Since Confederation, twenty-four have been given to the Western provinces and six to Newfoundland to make a total of one hundred and two members. While the Senate thus represents the provinces to some extent, it has never really acted as a protector of provincial rights. As we shall see later, the provinces have been more adequately protected by the very nature of Canadian federalism, and by their own exertions, than they have been by the Senate. Nevertheless, the smaller provinces, and even more so Quebec, feel that there

---

*Not to be confused with "private members' bills," that is, bills introduced by private members rather than the government, such as the bill in 1960 to abolish capital punishment brought down by the Member for Scarborough, Frank McGee. These bills seldom pass unless the government decides to back them.

is a definite place for the Senate, and that on minor issues
or in time of crisis it might serve a useful purpose.

Reform or Abolition?

However, some critics persist in believing that the Senate
should be abolished. Indeed, almost since 1867 opposition
parties have advocated its abolition, only to forget their
proposals when in office. The abolitionists argue that an
appointed legislative body is undemocratic, that nothing
should stand in the way of the will of the people as expressed through their elected representatives in the Commons, and that if the Senate does not really interfere or
seriously affect Commons' decisions then it is superfluous
anyway and might as well be abolished. As we have seen,
however, in checking the details of legislation and discussing private bills, the Senate does perform useful work.

Many Canadians, while not believing in abolition of the
Senate, urge that it be reformed in some way. The most
common proposals and arguments are these:

1.   Younger men should be appointed. This was par-

"Shouldn't Be Long: Can't Stay On Their Feet More Than 10 Minutes"

ticularly crucial before legislation passed in 1965 made retirement compulsory at 75. Nonetheless, the average
Senator is appointed in his late fifties and the average age
of Senators is well over sixty, so that some members are too
old to do any work. Whether many young men would want
to accept such an appointment is, however, debatable and
might depend on whether the Senate was given greater
status and importance.

2.   The Senate should cease to be a political pasture,
the "House of the political dead" as the political scientist
Goldwin Smith long ago sarcastically described it. It is
generally conceded that the great political value of the
Senate is that it provides a useful form of patronage. Defeated Members of the Commons, loyal party supporters in
the business world, disappointed cabinet candidates and
others may be rewarded with a post in the Senate. Reform-
ers urge that appointments should be made from among
non-political people such as journalists, civil servants, military men, teachers, scientists, professors, etc., so that the
Senate might represent a wider cross-section of the nation.
The recent appointments of Eugene Forsey, a scholar and
labour official, and Ernest Manning, the long-time Premier
of Alberta, have not only added talent and experience, but
broken a pattern of partisan appointments.

In opposition almost every party has pleaded the case
for Senate reform. Yet in office they act quite differently.
Before their re-election in 1963 many Liberals were heard
to argue the case for this type of Senate reform. During
their first two years in power, however, the Liberals appointed nine new Senators: seven were prominent and
wealthy Liberals who had served the party well in fund-
raising and party organization; one was an M.P. (largely
remembered for his annual speeches against goof balls)
who had resigned his seat to enable a cabinet aspirant to
run in a safe riding; and the last was another M.P. whose
inept performance in the Commons earned him a seat in
the Red Chamber, as the Senate is called. Even a member
of the C.C.F., which, like the present N.D.P., advocated
abolition of the Senate, once admitted that when elected
". . . the first thing we would have to do would be to get

somebody in the Senate to represent us there . . . and once having embarked upon that course we probably might consider changing our policy of abolition."

3.   More severe rules should be imposed regarding attendance and participation. At present too many Senators simply make a formal appearance to enjoy the "club" and pick up their cheques. Of one Senator *The Ottawa Citizen* wrote on April 21, 1930:

> Senator Dessaules, dead at St. Hyacinthe, who held a seat in the Senate of Canada since 1907, had a remarkable record. So far as is recalled by those around the Senate since he was there, he never once participated in any debate or gave expression to an opinion; but he followed the discussions closely and was there when the division bells rang. He was a kindly old man, held by all parties in venerable respect because of his great age.

4.   Better use could be made of the talent in the Senate by giving it major committee and research assignments such as those on Manpower, problems of credit purchasing, and the recent study of Hate Propaganda.

5.   The Senate should be an elected chamber like the American Senate. Such a proposal, perhaps, raises more problems than it solves. Do we need two elected chambers? Would they be in conflict? Or would both be dominated by the Cabinet? What would happen if the Cabinet was defeated in one but not in the other House? Would it have to resign as it does now after defeat in the Commons?

6.   The most common modern approach is to make the Senate more effectively represent the provinces. In the discussions of constitutional reform that have been held since 1968, the federal government and most of the provinces have recommended that the provincial governments appoint some members of the Senate. Endorsing this principle, the federal government added that "a reconstituted Senate should have certain special powers flowing from its role as an important institution of federalism. It should have a new jurisdiction to approve nominations by the federal government of judges of the Supreme Court of

Canada, ambassadors and heads of cultural agencies. For the same reason it should be considered to have a special responsibility in dealing with legislative measures concerning official languages and human rights." Since this approach to Senate reform is one of the least controversial matters facing the Constitutional Conferences (see pages 118-21), it is highly likely that Senate reform along these lines will soon be accomplished.

Yet reform of the Senate has in the past always been talked about and never implemented. The government enjoys the patronage. Party war-horses look forward to their retirement in the Red Chamber. The public is generally indifferent, and has exerted little pressure for reform. The tragedy is that a body of one hundred and two intelligent, experienced, and dedicated men and women could perform far more valuable services for the country than the Senate does at present, or is likely to do if the only change is to spread the power of appointment among eleven governments.

5 PARLIAMENT AND THE PRESS

The House of Commons debates are printed and published every day. Known as *Hansard*, the debates may be purchased for three dollars a year. However, few Canadians read the debates, and generally the copies merely gather dust on library shelves. Most citizens depend upon daily newspapers and radio and television stations for information about what is going on in Parliament. The mass media, therefore, is really an essential part of the governmental process. Indeed, the press has been regarded as so important that some writers have referred to it as the fourth branch of the government. For this reason some discussion of the press and other news media is essential in any study of Canadian government and politics.

Although Canadian journalism and broadcasting is generally of a high quality, there are some aspects which disturb thoughtful observers. Most newspapers today tend on the whole to take a partisan point of view in politics and support one political party. This partisanship is acceptable in editorials and in signed columns, which everyone clearly understands to be statements of opinion. But people believe that news coverage should be objective and free from partisanship. Many critics of the press contend that newspapers do publish politically partisan news, or sometimes select and locate news stories with something less than complete impartiality.

The newspapers vigorously deny such charges. Yet readers of the Toronto Press know that the *Telegram* and *The Globe and Mail* openly support the Conservative Party (except on rare occasions like the election of 1963). On the other hand, the *Toronto Star* is openly Liberal. In Ottawa the *Citizen* is an ardent editorial supporter of the Liberals while the *Journal* is one of the most enthusiastic Conservative journals in Canada. Most newspapers in Canada can

Two Toronto dailies, one Liberal and one Conservative, reported that the Diefenbaker government had encountered a serious financial crisis and had had to borrow money abroad to avoid collapse of the nation's financial system. The headlines intentionally gave a different view of the crisis.

be labelled with similar clarity. Few Canadians question this kind of political affiliation, believing that Canadian public life would be less vital with complete editorial objectivity. Political affiliation should not affect or distort a newspaper's coverage and presentation of the news. But *does* it?

Most newspapers would reply with a categorical No. But Pierre Berton, writing in the *Toronto Star* on June 14, 1962, declared that during the election campaign of that year *The Globe and Mail* had given the Conservatives 2,823 column inches and the Liberals 2,122, while the *Telegram* gave the Conservatives 3,535 inches to the Liberals' 2,080. On the other hand, the *Star* gave the Tories 2,695 and the Liberals 3,200 column inches. "These are the figures," wrote Berton. "Make of them what you will."

Two University of Waterloo scholars using a research staff and a computer did a more detailed examination of the Ontario press during the same election campaign. They also found a sharp difference between the extent and nature of the coverage given the different parties, in both news and editorial columns, by newspapers of different political persuasions. The authors observed: "The issues which concerned the *Telegram* illustrate its role not merely as a reporter, but also as a partisan in the campaign. . . . Like the *Telegram*, the *Toronto Star* was unashamedly partisan, perhaps in many respects even more so. . . . The *Globe* did favour the Conservatives, but the partisanship was less marked than in any other metropolitan newspaper." The authors did not recommend complete nonpartisanship, but did conclude, "We would, however, perhaps like to see papers admit more readily to partisanship and not try to disguise bias as objectivity."*

There is not yet the close affiliation between a political party and a radio or T.V. station that there is between newspapers and parties. But the same principles should apply. Editorials should be clearly designated as such, while the selection and presentation of the news should be completely objective and impartial. Just as a teacher of history should make clear where his statements of fact end and his personal beliefs begin, so should radio and television news commentators.

Many Canadians are less concerned about the partisanship of newspapers in their support of rival political parties than they are about the press generally reflecting only one side of the political scene. They argue that it really matters very little whether a paper supports the Liberals or the Conservatives, or whether its news columns give more space to the favoured party or not. Their main concern is that generally only *one* side of the political spectrum—the centre or right of centre—receives sympathetic coverage in the press.

Ownership of the Press

One reason for this tendency of the press to reflect only one side of the political scene is that it is a very expensive undertaking to establish and operate a major newspaper or a private radio or T.V. station. The day when a journalist could open up a newspaper in a small town virtually out

Papers on the 1962 Election, John Meisel, ed. University of Toronto Press. By permission of the publishers.

of a suitcase is gone. Today millions of dollars are needed. Ownership of the mass media is like the ownership of other multi-million dollar businesses. A glance at *Who's Who* will reveal that the men who own the daily papers—or, as we shall see, the chains of daily newspapers and the major radio and T.V. stations or chains—are indistinguishable in many ways from the men who control the industrial and financial structure of the country. On the whole, such men support the status quo and stand in the centre or to the right of centre on the political spectrum. They are generally conservative in their approach to economic and social questions.

Most experts on the press refer to this fact. Louis Lyons of Harvard University stated in a speech in Toronto in 1962 that the press is a one-party press, meaning a press with a generally conservative point of view. "The publisher, a big business man, has the same stake as other business men, on one side of issues of taxes and wages, budgets and trade unions. This is the basic nature of the press. It is a business." In a study of the press in Canada, Carlton McNaught emphasized the same point: ". . . the publisher often acquires a point of view which is that of the business groups in the community rather than of other and perhaps opposed groups; and this point of view is more likely than not to be reflected in his paper's treatment of news. The publisher usually belongs to the same clubs, moves in the same social circles, and breathes the same atmosphere as other business men."* In his book, *The Vertical Mosaic*, Professor John Porter, a Carleton University sociologist, reached the same conclusions in a thorough study of the ownership of the press: "The ideological orientation that results from the existing pattern of ownership is conservative, supporting the status quo over a wide range of social and economic policy."

Under the circumstances it is not surprising that there is no major socialist daily newspaper in Canada, nor even a daily that supports the N.D.P. It is true that the *Toronto*

Canada Gets the News, Carleton McNaught, The Ryerson Press. By permission of the publishers.

Star has taken a left-of-centre position on many public issues, and *The Vancouver Sun* at times has adopted the same position. And other papers like the Toronto *Telegram* have columnists representing a wide variety of political beliefs. Furthermore, many reporters do not share the views of the editors or owners and, on many papers, are given considerable freedom. Nevertheless, on the whole, the press does reflect an acceptance of the status quo, does reflect one side of the political scene. To suggest, as it has been suggested, that a conservative newspaper alters its nature by employing a socialist columnist is to argue that to place a Druid in the middle of the Sahara transforms the desert into a grove of English oaks.

Another matter of increasing concern in recent years has been the concentration of ownership of the press and, perhaps even more serious, the growing trend towards newspaper control of radio and T.V. stations. The information on pages 91-3, drawn largely from the Report of the Special Senate Committee on Mass Media in 1970, gives some indication of what has happened and what is happening in Canada. Before the First World War there were 138 newspapers in Canada and 138 publishers; today 12 publishing groups produce more than two-thirds of the country's 116 dailies. These groups control more than 75 per cent of daily circulation, with only the French press in Quebec and Nova Scotia falling significantly below that figure.

Most observers—in Canada, Great Britain and the United States—are concerned about such concentration of ownership, and find the present trends unsettling, if not dangerous. Canadian observers are concerned that almost half of the daily papers read in English-speaking Canada are published by three firms—Southam, F. P. Publications and Thomson—controlled by a handful of men. There is a widespread concern about the one-newspaper town, or the cities like Charlottetown, Victoria, Saint John and Thunder Bay, where two newspapers, however different and competitive in theory, are in the final analysis under the same ownership. Referring to a basically one-newspaper town, the editor of the *Troy Record* in New York said a number of years ago:

What then becomes of freedom of the press? It represents in this city my right—or if he wishes to exercise it, the publisher's—to say my say. If I wish to be decent enough I can let people write me letters on the other side; but I don't have to do this. Nobody can speak his mind in Troy except on the platform or on my say-so. . . . As a matter of fact, because we believe in the freedom of the press, we open our columns willingly to the other side. But this makes freedom of the press less a constitutional right than a privilege we graciously grant to the other fellow.*

1. *The Southam Press*

Daily papers owned or controlled: (circ. 850,000)	*The Ottawa Citizen, The Hamilton Spectator, North Bay Nugget, Winnipeg Tribune, Medicine Hat News, The Calgary Herald, Edmonton Journal, Prince George Citizen, Vancouver Province, Owen Sound Sun Times*
Daily papers partially owned:	*London Free Press, Kitchener-Waterloo Record, Brandon Sun*
Weeklies:	*Financial Times, News and Chronicle*
Magazines:	Over fifty, including 50 per cent interest in *The Canadian* and *The Canadian Star Weekly*
Radio and T.V.:	Ownership, control or interest in twenty-seven

2. *Sifton-Bell (F. P. Publications)*

Daily papers owned or controlled: (circ. 855,000)	Toronto *Globe and Mail*, *Winnipeg Free Press*, Ottawa *Journal*, *Calgary Albertan*, *Lethbridge Herald*, *Victoria Daily Colonist*, *Victoria Daily Times*, *The Vancouver Sun*
Radio and T.V.:	Two cable stations

*By permission of the publishers, *The Record Newspapers*.

3. *Sifton Group*

Daily papers owned or controlled:	Regina *Leader-Post, Saskatoon Star-Phoenix*
Radio and T.V.:	Ownership, control or interest in six radio and T.V. stations

4. *Thomson Newspapers*
(circ. 400,000)

Owns [1970] thirty newspapers, including both the Charlottetown newspapers and the Thunder Bay papers, eleven weeklies and until 1970 had interests in ten Ontario radio and T.V. stations, which it sold to Bushnell.

5. *K. C. Irving*

Daily papers owned or controlled:	Saint John *Telegraph-Journal*, Saint John *Times-Globe*, Moncton *Times*, Moncton *Transcript*, Fredericton *Gleaner*. (There are only five English-language dailies in New Brunswick!)
Radio and T.V.:	Three

6. *Desmarais-Parisien-Francoeur* (*previously the Power Corporation holdings*)

Daily papers owned or controlled:	Montreal *La Presse*, Sherbrooke *La Tribune*, Three Rivers *Le Nouvelliste*, Granby *La Voix de l'Est*
Weeklies:	Seventeen
Radio and T.V.:	Three

7. *Bassett-Eaton*

Daily papers owned or controlled:	Toronto *Telegram*
Weeklies:	Seven
T.V.:	Two

8. *Bushnell Communications*

Radio and T.V.:	Twelve radio and ten T.V.

9. *Maclean-Hunter*
   Weeklies: *Financial Post*
   Magazines: Over sixty including *Maclean's* and *Chatelaine*
   Radio and T.V.: Twenty-one

10. *Toronto Star Ltd.*
    Daily papers owned or controlled: Toronto *Star*, Oakville *Daily Journal Record*
    Weeklies: Eleven plus 50 per cent of *The Canadian* and *The Canadian Star Weekly*
    Radio and T.V.: Unsuccessful applicant for T.V. licence

The Special Senate Committee Report had words of praise for some Canadian newspapers, but in general it was highly critical of the service the press and media gave in return for the large profits they usually secured.

> In a few cases, the corporations concerned are making genuine efforts to deliver quality editorial content and quality programming in return for their privileged economic position. But the general pattern, unfortunately, is of newspapers and broadcasting stations that are pulling the maximum out of their communities, and giving back the minimum in return. This is what, in contemporary parlance, is called a rip-off.
>
> In traditional usage, you have a monopoly rip-off when the corporations concerned use their privileged position to charge their customers more than the traffic would otherwise bear. In the case of the press today, we think, the problem is reversed: it's not that the companies are charging too much, but that they're spending too little. Many Canadian daily newspapers could readily afford to develop their own editorial-page columnists, their own cartoonists, their own commentators. But it's cheaper, far cheaper, to buy syndicated American columnists and reprint other papers' cartoons, and to skimp on news coverage in the hope that one of the wire services will do the job.

The Senate Committee Report recognized, however, that

chain ownership of the press did provide some advantages. "Although chain ownership can lead to the sort of numbing journalistic conformity that characterizes the Thomson newspapers, it can also confer benefits that are unquestionably in the public interest," noted the Report. "The most compelling benefit, of course, is that group ownership tends to prevent more newspapers from dying. When two group-owned dailies are competing in the same town, the result is usually a "truce" instead of a winner-take-all struggle for circulation. In Vancouver, it is probable that the smaller of the city's two dailies, the *Province*, would have folded years ago if it weren't for the fact that two large groups jointly own the company that publishes both papers. The same can be said of . . . Winnipeg and Ottawa."

Nevertheless, the Committee urged the federal government to establish a Press Ownership Review Board with power to approve or disapprove of new mergers or acquisitions of newspapers and periodicals. The Board, said the Report, "should have one basic guideline, spelled out in its enabling legislation: *all* transactions that increase concentration of ownership in the mass media are undesirable and contrary to the public interest—unless shown to be otherwise." The Committee also recommended that the government establish a $2 million Publications Development Loan Fund to assist what it called the "Volkswagen Press," the small weeklies or monthlies, like *Dimension, Last Post, The Mysterious East, The 4th Estate* and others, which have a no-holds-barred editorial and reporting policy. These publications are usually far left of centre, highly critical of the status quo, and find it difficult to attract advertising, but they help to provide both a challenge to the large newspapers and a variety of news analysis and opinion.

Even more disturbing, perhaps, than the concentration of control over the press is the tendency of the press to move into ownership and control of radio and T.V. There is a natural connection between the two developments, and joint control is increasing dramatically in Canada. Publishing giants are becoming broadcasting giants. In 1962 there were eight Canadian cities where the newspaper and the

T.V. station were under the same ownership, and the figures may well have risen. In London, Ontario, for example, the *London Free Press*, radio station CFPL, and CFPL-T.V. are controlled by the same family, and the giant Southam chain has minority interests in all.

Like many of the experts, the Board of Broadcast Governors has also tended to regard this interlocking ownership as dangerous. As John Cartwright wrote in the *Canadian Commentator* in 1962: "In case anyone should accuse newspaper publishers of a shameful lack of enterprise for only controlling 20 per cent of their greatest rival's private outlets, it should be remembered that the Board of Broadcast Governors has seemed to regard giving television franchises to newspaper owners as somewhat akin to giving an extra tentacle to an octopus in a tankful of goldfish." In recent years the Canadian Radio-Television Commission, which controls radio and T.V. licensing, has continued to look critically on mixed press and media ownership and has generally followed the view that such concentration is bad unless proved otherwise.

The reasons for the growth of concentration in the mass media field are economic. There is no apparent disposition on the part of the chains to manipulate or control thought or information. Yet the *potential* dangers have disturbed many Canadians. Aware of this public reaction, the Southam press apparently decided a few years ago to divest itself of majority interest in radio stations in those towns where it had a monopoly newspaper. And at the moment the Board of Broadcast Governors in Canada is following the lead of a Royal Commission in Britain and is studying the extent and effects of the ownership of one medium by another. Presumably, at some future date public regulations will define the line between economic necessity or desirability and the public good.

Pressure on the Press

Another question raised in every book and every conference on the press concerns the effects on the quality and the freedom of the media of the dependence of newspapers and radio and T.V. stations on commercial advertising. As we know, the price we pay for the newspaper hardly covers the cost of its delivery to the door. The real costs are borne not by sales but by advertising. Advertising in turn is related to sales, for the larger the circulation or the audience the easier it is to secure advertising and the higher the charges can be.

One unquestioned effect of the interdependence of advertising and sales is that the media seek to appeal to the largest common denominator. Thus they tend to define news less in terms of the importance of the event than of the readership or audience it will attract. In this respect a grisly hometown murder may be "better news" than a crisis in the Middle East which could lead to a third world war. And since more people seem to prefer westerns to opera, or detective thrillers to more sophisticated drama, the radio and T.V. stations cater to the popular taste. Such popular programmes are easily sponsored, while a station may have to incur heavy losses to support the presentation of an opera or ballet. One of the major functions of the C.B.C. is to use the taxpayers' dollars to present programmes which could not be afforded by a commercial station dependent on advertising revenue to meet its costs and provide a normal business profit.

A charge often made against the press is that dependence on advertising destroys or limits its freedom. Critics have suggested that newspapers or radio and T.V. stations may well be reluctant to adopt editorial positions or publish sensitive news items for fear of antagonizing major advertisers. This subject, wrote a British journalist, is "one of the most frequent questions at any meeting where newspapers are discussed." Newspapermen indignantly deny that their papers have ever submitted to pressure from an advertiser, although they usually concede that it has or may have happened to others. There is no doubt that the large and powerful Canadian dailies should be able to withstand pressure from even the largest advertiser, for the advertiser needs the paper as much as the paper needs the advertiser.

On the other hand, there are indications that advertising influence is not entirely absent. Kingsley Martin (an Englishman) and Curtis McDougall (an American) refer to copy labelled "B.O. Must" (Business Office Must) which originates in the advertising department and which "indicates" to other departments that certain firms are looked upon favourably.* More serious was the charge made years ago that the American press was very reluctant to give any coverage to the medical research which linked smoking and lung diseases.

On the whole it would seem that the Canadian press is happily less responsive to such pressure than the American, or even the British, press. But Douglas Fisher, at the time an M.P., was not contradicted when he declared that editors of two papers were present when remarks critical of forestry policy were made and "came to me separately and suggested that printing the facts might shake public confidence in the industry. In the end neither paper carried anything."** Mr. Fisher stated that reporters on these papers had told him that "they have orders never to be critical of paper mills or other large business interests without first consulting their publishers."†

Such comments by responsible members of the Canadian community serve to keep alive the doubts about complete media independence from advertiser or business interests, and to make some people sceptical about the denials of publishers and broadcasters. During the 1965 election campaign, doubts were intensified when the CTV television network refused to broadcast a paid political advertisement by the N.D.P. dealing with what the N.D.P. felt was misleading advertising. Although Dr. Andrew Stewart of the Board of Broadcast Governors considered the party's advertisement acceptable, network officials declared that it represented an indiscriminate attack on T.V. advertising and was itself misleading.†† CTV may have been right, but some Canadians wondered whether the network showed the same concern for the consumer when it screened T.V. commercials as it did for advertisers when it screened the N.D.P. advertisement.

---

*Kingsley Martin, *The Press the Public Wants*, Hogarth Press, London, 1947; and Curtis McDougall, *The Press and its Problems*, Dubuque, 1964.
**The Globe and Mail*, February 19, 1962.
†*The Montreal Star*, February 19, 1962.
††*The Globe and Mail*, October 23, 1965.

So far little mention has been made of the Canadian Broadcasting Corporation, owned by the people of Canada. While the C.B.C. is dependent on advertising for part of its revenue, it does not permit sponsored news or public affairs programmes. Nor, as a matter of policy, does it let personal views creep into the presentation of the news although the practice is almost impossible to enforce. On the whole, most Canadians would agree that C.B.C. public affairs and news programmes are designed to enlighten rather than to persuade. Complete objectivity and impartiality is impossible. In determining the content of news items and how to read them there is always an element of subjectivity. But there is a good deal of difference between subjective decisions made with objectivity as the goal, and subjectivity or editorializing as an end in itself. To the extent that individual members of the C.B.C. staff forget that impartiality and enlightenment are their goal, rather than editorializing and moulding opinion, they are violating the only valid objective for news and public affairs programming by a publicly owned system.

This discussion of the press has taken us a long way from Parliament. But to the extent that one of the major functions of the House of Commons is to act as a public forum, we should be as concerned about the health of the institutions through which we receive the news and by which our ideas are moulded, as we are about the health of Parliament itself.

6 OTTAWA AND THE PROVINCES

Canada is a federal state or a federation, that is, a country in which power to legislate, or make law, is divided between a national government and provincial or state governments. In Canada this distribution of authority is set out in a written document, the British North America Act of 1867, and neither of the governments can invade the sphere of power reserved to the other without consent.

The Nature of Canadian Federalism

Every federal state represents a compromise between the desire of a number of regions to preserve their own existence and the desire or need for unity among them. The exact form that the federation takes will reflect the relative strength of these two desires. In the United States, after the American Revolution, local feelings were very strong, and so outweighed the desire for unity that the federation was weak. The new central, or federal, government was given a minimum of power, while the states retained a great deal of authority.

In the British North American colonies a century ago, when statesmen were planning a union, the need was clearly for a strong central government. All the colonies faced serious economic hardship which they could not overcome by themselves. A strong national government was necessary to encourage trade between the colonies and with the outside world, and to build railways and canals to transport their goods. The Canadians cast envious eyes upon the Western prairies with their opportunities for large and prosperous settlements. But the West had to be purchased from the Hudson's Bay Company and railways had to be built to cement a nation that was to stretch from sea to sea. Only a strong central government could pursue a vigorous policy of expansion and nation-building. Fear of

the United States persuaded many Canadians that only a
strong national government could organize suitable methods of national defence.

Even if these factors were not enough to overcome the
intense desire of Maritimers and *Québecois* to retain their
local autonomy, there was yet another, and perhaps more
conclusive, reason for creating a strong central government. Just as the colonies in British North America were
beginning to consider federation, the American union was
ripped and ravaged by the Civil War. As reports of the
slaughter were spread across their newspapers, Canadians
believed that the Civil War could have been prevented if
the central government had been stronger. Here, the dangers of a weak federation were starkly displayed for all to
see. Thus Canadians decided to construct a highly centralized federal state in which the balance of power rested
heavily on the side of the national government.

Distribution of Powers

The central feature of every federal system and the best
illustration of the balance of power within it is the division
of law-making power between the central and provincial
governments. In the British North America Act of 1867,
the Fathers of Confederation gave the main powers of
government to the Dominion and left only local and minor
matters to the provinces. The provincial powers were listed
in Section 92 of the Act and all other powers rested with
the federal government. In addition to this *residual* authority, twenty-nine examples of the federal power were listed
for purposes of illustration, as the comparative table on
pages 102-3 shows.

It is clear that the central government was given the
major responsibilities and the main sources of revenue,
indeed any source of revenue it chose to use. Direct taxation, such as income tax, was hardly thought of at that
time and the provinces were in great part dependent upon
annual grants from Ottawa to finance their affairs. This
system of federal financial assistance was another striking
illustration of where the balance of power lay.

Two other sections of the British North America Act

"Making the greatest show on earth of themselves" was the caption
Bengough gave to his 1895 cartoon. In 1890 Manitoba had abolished
separate schools and, after years of delay, the Conservative government in Ottawa issued a remedial order demanding that the province
restore the rights of the minority. Manitoba bluntly refused to obey
the order, however, and the government, led by Mackenzie Bowell
(centre), was sharply divided itself. Finally, in 1896, the government
attempted to secure the passage of a remedial bill, but Liberals and
anti-remedial Conservatives engaged in a prolonged and successful
filibuster. The Conservatives were defeated by Laurier in the election
that followed soon afterwards, and the Liberal Prime Minister pursued
a policy of diplomacy rather than coercion to persuade Manitoba to
restore some of the rights of the Roman Catholic minority there.

were important and interesting for the future of dominion-
provincial relations. Section 95 gave both the provinces
and the Dominion authority to legislate on agriculture and
immigration, but provided that if there were ever a clash
between them on those matters, the Dominion laws would

THE DISTRIBUTION OF

DOMINION POWERS

91. It shall be lawful for the Queen, by and with the Advice and Consent of the Senate and House of Commons, to make Laws for the Peace, Order, and good Government of Canada, in relation to all Matters not coming within the Classes of Subjects by this Act assigned exclusively to the Legislatures of the Provinces; . . .

ILLUSTRATIONS:

1. The Public Debt and Property
2. The Regulation of Trade and Commerce
3. The raising of Money by any Mode or System of Taxation
5. The Postal Service
7. Militia, Military and Naval Service, and Defence
10. Navigation and Shipping
12. Sea Coast and Inland Fisheries
14. Currency and Coinage
15. Banking . . . and the Issue of Paper Money
24. Indians and Lands reserved for Indians
25. Naturalization and Aliens
26. Marriage and Divorce
27. The Criminal Law

LEGISLATIVE POWER

PROVINCIAL POWERS

92. In each Province the Legislature may exclusively make Laws in relation to Matters coming within the Classes of Subjects next hereinafter enumerated; that is to say:
    1. The Amendment from Time to Time . . . of the Constitution of the Province, except as regards the Office of Lieutenant-Governor
    2. Direct Taxation within the Province in order to the Raising of a Revenue for Provincial Purposes
    5. The Management and Sale of the Public Lands belonging to the Province and of the Timber and Wood thereon
    8. Municipal Institutions in the Province
    9. Shop, Saloon, Tavern, Auctioneer, and other licences
    10. Local Works and Understakings other than such as are of the following Classes:
        a) Transportation facilities linking two provinces
        b) Transportation facilities linking Canada and other countries
        c) Facilities which the Parliament of Canada declares to be for the welfare of Canada or more than the single province
    12. The Solemnization of Marriage in the Province
    13. Property and Civil rights in the Province
    14. The Administration of Justice . . .
    16. Generally all Matters of a merely local or private Nature in the Province
93. In and for each Province the legislature may exclusively make laws in relation to Education. . . .

be supreme. Section 93 gave the provinces complete control over education, but the federal government was
charged with protecting the rights of religious minorities if
they were interfered with by the provincial government. It
has attempted to do this only once—during the celebrated
Manitoba School Question controversy in the 1890's—and
then was only partially successful.

Control over the Provinces

The Fathers of Confederation were not content only to
endow the federal government with the major tasks and
revenues. They also sought to give the central government some control over the activities of the provinces. For
this reason, the Lieutenant-Governor was made a federal
officer, appointed by, paid by and liable to dismissal by the
central government. He was given the power to reserve
bills for the consideration of the federal Cabinet, which
could then allow the bill to become law or not, as it saw fit.
The Lieutenant-Governor was also to keep Ottawa informed of all that was going on in the province and, when
necessary, to pass on advice or warnings from Ottawa to
his government. In one draft of the British North America
Act the Lieutenant-Governor was called the Superinten-
dent, a word that clearly shows how the Fathers of Confederation regarded his function. Moreover, the federal
government was given the power of disallowance. The
Lieutenant-Governor was to send every provincial statute
to Ottawa. Within one year the federal government could
disallow the measure if it felt that it was not in the national
interest.

The provinces were given authority over the administration of justice, but the federal government possessed the
authority to appoint judges as well as to control the criminal law. This permitted the central government to maintain
some measure of control over the judicial system. As we
have seen, too, the federal Cabinet was given power to
appoint members of the Senate, an arrangement deliberately aimed at weakening the Senate's role as a protector of
provincial rights.

In short, the Fathers of Confederation created a highly

centralized federal system. They did it deliberately because
they realized that local feelings were too strong to enable
them to form one united country without any provincial or
state divisions, and they accepted confederation as a necessary compromise. As Sir John A. Macdonald declared,
when appealing to his fellow Canadians to accept the proposal for a federation:

> Ever since the [American] union was formed the diffi-
> culty of what is called "State Rights" has existed, and
> this had much to do with bringing on the present un-
> happy war in the United States. They commenced, in
> fact, at the wrong end. . . . Here we have adopted a
> different system. We have strengthened the General
> Government. We have given the General Legislature
> all the great subjects of legislation. . . . We have thus
> avoided that great source of weakness which has been
> the cause of the disruption of the United States. We
> have avoided all conflict of jurisdiction and authority.

Macdonald was too optimistic. Canada has never had a
civil war, it is true, but there have been many conflicts of
authority between the provinces and the central government. Canadian federalism has moved far away from the
intentions of the Fathers of Confederation in the direction
of decentralization or greater provincial rights and powers.

What Has Happened to Canadian Federalism?

Only a detailed study of Canadian history could tell us
what has happened to Canadian federalism since Confederation in 1867. Here, we will merely outline some general
developments which have played an important role in the
changing relationships of the central and provincial governments. Most people would point first to the courts as
being primarily responsible for the shift in power that has
taken place. In any federal system, it is not always certain
whether a given matter falls within the federal or provincial sphere of authority. The ultimate decision rests with
the courts which must interpret the constitution. Until
1949, when the Supreme Court of Canada became the last
court of appeal, the final decision in Canadian cases rested
with the Judicial Committee of the Privy Council, a court

which sat in London, England. The Judicial Committee judges consistently showed sympathy for the provinces in upholding and extending provincial rights; they seemed little in favour of championing federal power. Historians, lawyers and political scientists argue to this day whether the Privy Council's decisions were correct, but the fact remains that the court seriously limited federal authority and gave "property and civil rights" (a provincial power) a very broad meaning. Perhaps the best expression of the Judicial Committee's view came from Lord Watson who declared in 1892 that the object of the British North America Act was "neither to weld the provinces into one, nor to subordinate provincial governments to a central authority." Yet unless we have completely misinterpreted our history, and unless we cannot believe what the Fathers of Confederation said, we know that the object of the Act *was* pre-

THE NEW IDEA OF CONFEDERATION.

As early as 1879 when this cartoon appeared in **Grip** there was opposition to the strongly centralized federal system which had been established in 1867. John A. Macdonald is shown here turning the handle of the merry-go-round while the provincial premiers enjoy the "no provincial autonomy" ride.

cisely to subordinate provincial governments to a central authority!

The second major cause of decentralization has been a change in opinion among the Canadian people themselves. The circumstances of the 1860's, as we have seen, demanded a strong central government. But the citizens of the new nation remained firm in their loyalty to their provinces and were Canadians only secondarily. It was to be a long time—and the process is by no means yet complete—before the people of Canada gave their first loyalty to the nation. Thus, as conditions changed, as the fear of the United States lessened and as the federal government failed to bring the anticipated prosperity to the country, the old provincial loyalties began to reassert themselves. Men from all parts of Canada began to resent the supremacy of the government at Ottawa and sought to increase provincial powers.

Led by Oliver Mowat, its Premier for twenty-four years, Ontario began a concerted attack on the federal power of disallowance, the position of the Lieutenant-Governor as a federal officer and the distribution of legislative authority. Manitoba successfully challenged the power of disallowance in the 1890's. The Maritime provinces campaigned for, and won, better financial terms, sometimes aided by the powerful voice of Quebec and a less powerful echo from British Columbia. The Conservative Party under Sir John A. Macdonald remained faithful to the original design, but the Liberals, under Edward Blake and Wilfrid Laurier, championed provincial rights. When the Liberals won the election of 1896, it was in part a victory for provincial rights.

More important than either the judicial or political causes, however, was the changing conception of the functions of government which accompanied the changes in Canada's economy. In the early years of the twentieth century, Canada became increasingly industrialized. The cities encroached rapidly on the countryside. Men left the farms to work in the factories, where they were no longer their own employers but became dependent upon others for work. These changes created social problems—problems of

Adrift on a Stormy Sea

The Depression led to the appointment of the first great Royal Commission on federal-provincial relations, popularly known as the Rowell-Sirois Commission, members of which cartoonist Arch Dale has put on the raft. After intensive research and study the Commission reported that the provinces should surrender some of their taxation powers to the federal government, which in return should assume provincial debts, the responsibility for unemployment relief, and the obligation to provide a minimum standard of living for everyone in Canada by providing the poorer provinces with "national adjustment grants." The recommendations were immediately opposed by the richer provinces. While little came of the recommendations at the time, they were instituted, in one way or another, after the Second World War.

health, welfare and unemployment—which demanded government action. In addition, the automobile made necessary the construction of tens and then hundreds of thousands of miles of highways. Progressive thinking resulted in the introduction of *free* education from kindergarten to the end of high school, as well as substantial government sup-

port for university education. The responsibility for providing and financing all these services, which no one had
dreamed of in 1867, fell to the provinces. At the same
time, however, provincial revenues had not increased pro-
portionately.

This imbalance between responsibilities and revenues
was starkly revealed by the Depression of the 1930's. Virtually bankrupt or impoverished provinces could not provide relief for the hundreds of thousands of unemployed, or
in some cases look after the ill and aged or even pay the
teachers in the schools. The federal government had more
funds but had no responsibility and, said the courts, no
power to act even in such an emergency. It was clear that
there would have to be a major overhaul of the Canadian
federal system to meet changed conditions—or at least it
should have been clear.

The Contemporary Problem

Since the Depression, federal and provincial statesmen,
who at times have resembled rival warlords, a number of
Royal Commissions and innumerable committees and conferences have wrestled with the dilemma of Canadian federalism. Discussions have focussed on five general and
interwoven considerations: the need for the federal government to maintain as high a level of employment and prosperity as possible and avoid another depression; the
necessity to provide the provinces with sufficient revenue to
meet their rapidly increasing responsibilities; the need to
equalize as much as possible the standard of living of all
Canadians regardless of where they live; the realization that
while many responsibilities are within the provincial legislative field they might better be handled on a national level;
and finally the possibility of a major reconstruction of the
constitution itself to make it a better instrument of government in the last half of the twentieth century.

The Depression underlined the need for government to
prevent such occurrences in the future if at all possible.
Led by Lord Keynes, economists maintained that it could
be done. What the government had to do, they said, was to
counter the ups and downs in the business cycle by use of

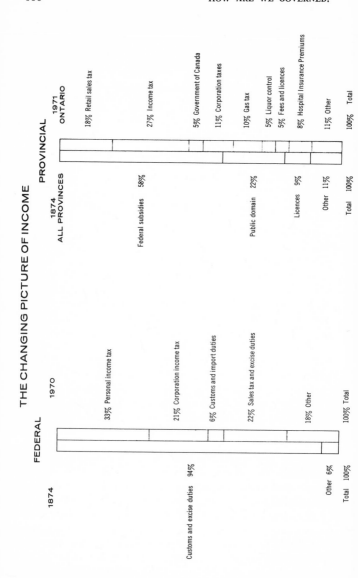

THE CHANGING PICTURE OF INCOME

FEDERAL

1874

Customs and excise duties   94%

Other   6%

Total   100%

1970

33% Personal income tax

21% Corporation income tax

6% Customs and import duties

22% Sales tax and excise duties

18% Other

100% Total

PROVINCIAL

1874
ALL PROVINCES

Federal subsidies   58%

Public domain   22%

Licences   9%

Other   11%

Total   100%

1971
ONTARIO

18% Retail sales tax

27% Income tax

5% Government of Canada

11% Corporation taxes

10% Gas tax

5% Liquor control

5% Fees and licences

8% Hospital Insurance Premiums

11% Other

100% Total

THE CHANGING PICTURE OF EXPENDITURE

FEDERAL

1874

Agriculture and lands 4%

Cost of government and justice 23%

Debt charges 27%

Defence 7%

Provincial subsidies 19%

Public welfare 1%

Transportation 17%

Other 2%

Total 100%

1970

16% Defence

19% Health and social security

14% Debt charges

9% Transportation and communications

10% Resources and industrial development

4% Veterans affairs

9% Payments to provinces

19% Other

100% Total

PROVINCIAL

1874 ALL PROVINCES

Agriculture and lands 9%

Cost of government 34%

Education 18%

Public welfare 8%

Transportation 15%

Other 16%

Total 100%

1971 ONTARIO

40% Education

13% Highways

22% Health and welfare

5% Resources

3% Public works

7% Municipal affairs

10% Other

100% Total

Knight Pearson begging Minister of Finance Gordon, "Quick, Walter, do something!"

Regardless of the party or Prime Minister in office, the federal-provincial battle over power and revenue goes on. In 1964 cartoonist Kuch of the **Winnipeg Free Press** used a medieval analogy, while in 1970 Macpherson of the **Toronto Star** and Donato of **The Toronto Telegram** went modern.

BUTCH BOURASSA and THE GUNDANCE KID

FEDERAL-PROVINCIAL FLIGHT NUMBER SIX, NOW BOARDING

its powers of taxing and spending. In good times it should raise taxes and save money. Then, when a recession threatened, it could spend money on public needs and projects and at the same time lower taxes, thus leaving the people with more to spend. These consumer expenditures would create a demand for goods and services which would counter the downward swing of the business cycle by maintaining production, employment and wages.

In a federal state, however, the theory was more easily stated than applied, for more than one government had powers of taxation and spending, and co-operation was necessary if the counter-cyclical policies were to work. The solution devised in Canada after the Second World War was for the provinces to rent their share of the major fields of taxation—personal and corporation income taxes and succession (death) duties—to the federal government, who then could control the taxation policy for the entire country. These *tax rental agreements* were renegotiated periodically. Naturally the provinces complained that they got too little, while the federal government insisted that it was paying too much.

In 1962 Prime Minister Diefenbaker's government abolished the agreements. Henceforth, the federal government was prepared to collect these taxes and return a certain percentage each year to the provinces. Any province that wished, or was obliged to, could levy its own tax in addition. The Prime Minister was convinced that "this new framework . . . should assure a new era of harmonious Dominion-Provincial fiscal relations. These proposals are new in spirit but rest upon the sound principles of financial responsibility and independence of governments." The *Canadian Tax Journal* was less enthusiastic: "Thus ends, in part, the bold post-war experiment to centralize major tax collections. The experiment had as one object the removal of differences in tax levels as a factor in the economic development of Canada and was intended as well to increase the effectiveness of the federal taxing power as a weapon to soften the ups and downs of our business and growth cycles."

The new arrangement did not inaugurate an harmonious era between Ottawa and the provinces. The latter continued to demand the return of a higher percentage to the provinces, while Ottawa repeatedly insisted that if the provinces needed more money they should increase taxes themselves. Indeed, as provincial expenditures increased every province raised one kind of tax after another. By 1971 all provinces except Ontario, British Columbia and Nova Scotia had added personal income taxes to those collected by the federal government. Unfortunately, it was usually the poorer provinces that were forced to levy the highest taxes to secure sufficient revenue to provide their residents with a decent standard of living and services.

The third consideration in the discussion of Canadian federalism is the desire to provide every Canadian with a minimum standard of living regardless of where he lives.

Since there are rich provinces and poor provinces in Canada, paradoxically the poor provinces have to levy higher taxes to provide even a lower standard of living than the rich provinces. Ever since Confederation the federal government had paid subsidies to the provinces, generally assisting the poor more than the rich. But in 1956 Ottawa formally endorsed a principle of equalization grants whereby it would pay the less affluent provinces a sum sufficient to enable them to provide a minimum level of provincial services without imposing a higher than normal rate of taxation.

In effect, equalization payments mean that residents of the richer provinces—Ontario, British Columbia and Alberta—are, through their taxes, assisting residents of the poorer regions. On the whole, the rich provinces have accepted the principle, although there have been occasional complaints that they were becoming the "milch cows" of Confederation. Justification for the principle of equalization, however, goes far beyond charity or a sense of the overall national interest. National economic policies have favoured some sections of Canada more than others. (The prairie farmer pays more for his Canadian-made truck because of a tariff which keeps out cheaper U.S. trucks, and therefore helps to support the eastern automobile industry.) Furthermore, wealth tends to be concentrated in the large eastern metropolitan centres of Ontario and Quebec and is therefore taxed there. Yet while the owners and directors of the large national banks, chain stores and industries tend to live in these two provinces, their profits are made by sales across the country. It may be argued, therefore, that the principle of some federal control over taxation and equalization payments is not only necessary but is also eminently just.

Another problem, again underlined by the Depression, was that human problems do not always respect provincial boundaries or the divisions of authority set down in the British North America Act. As thousands of unemployed wandered across the country in a desperate search for work or relief, it was obvious that unemployment relief had become a national problem. Yet the responsibility was provincial. This particular problem was eased in 1940 when an amendment to the B.N.A. Act gave the federal government responsibility for unemployment insurance. Many Canadians would argue, however, that illness, old age, education and many other matters in addition to unemployment also have no boundaries and that residents throughout Canada should enjoy at least a minimum level of services. The Trans-Canada Highway provides a different illustration of federal action in a traditionally provincial sphere; although highways are a provincial matter, the federal government took the initiative in encouraging the building of the road and financed much of its construction. Is it not fitting that the national government should do, in the age of the automobile, what it did in the railway age and build a concrete artery which, like the steel bands of the C.P.R. seventy-five years earlier, would make Canada a reality to its citizens?

The Trans-Canada Highway is an example of federal-provincial co-operation in what are known as *joint* or *shared-cost* programmes. These programmes have become the means whereby concerted national action can be taken in areas that legally fall within the jurisdiction of the provinces. Today there are dozens of such programmes: unemployment and old age assistance, hospital insurance and medicare, capital assistance to technical education and aid to university education, regional development and manpower training. As a rule, the federal government has taken the initiative in establishing the broad lines of policy, working out the details with the provinces, and paying a substantial part of the cost.

Most provinces have welcomed federal assistance, but they have not done so without qualifications. The chief criticisms are twofold. First: It has become apparent that what the federal government deems to be a national priority is not always regarded by the province involved as a matter of foremost concern. That is to say, Manitoba might feel that rather than invest in its share of a medicare programme it should give more money to education. Yet it is difficult to reject a proposal when some other government is willing to pay a major share of the cost. Second:

The poorer province finds it cannot always pay even the 10, 25 or 50 per cent of the cost of a joint programme. As Premier Robichaud of New Brunswick declared at the July 1965 Federal-Provincial Conference, his government was prepared to support the proposed medicare scheme "to the limit of our ability, but beg to point out the crucial importance of that qualification. Our ability, and the ability of several other provinces, is limited not by desire or intelligence but by dollars and cents."

While all provinces have pointed to the lack of consultation by Ottawa and the problems of priorities and financing, the most serious objection to joint programmes has come from the province of Quebec. When Maurice Duplessis was Premier (1936-39, 1944-59) the attitude of Quebec was completely negative. He opposed any encroachment of the federal government in the provincial sphere and refused any form of co-operation on the grounds that it would destroy provincial autonomy and French-Canadian culture. The nationalism of Premier Lesage, who was victorious in 1960, was no less intense but was much more positive. He agreed to participate in joint programmes to secure additional revenues, but warned that in the long run Quebec wanted to be *maître chez nous*, that is, to control all matters within provincial jurisdiction. By 1965 the pressure from Quebec for a new approach was successful. The federal government passed legislation permitting a province to *opt out* or *contract out* of any existing or new joint programme and still secure the equivalent federal contribution in cash. However, until the whole basis of federal-provincial financial relations was re-examined, Quebec, while administering the programmes from which it had opted out, had to maintain the level of services intended and was accountable to the federal government. Many of the other provincial premiers were not particularly happy with a move that could seriously weaken the central government, but all realized that opting out was one of the not unreasonable prices that had to be paid if the country were to solve the bicultural crisis.

Many people have argued that the only permanent solution to the problems of Canadian federalism is a major

TOWER OF LONDON

overhaul of the constitution and a clarification and re-
allocation of the federal and provincial taxing and spending powers. The solution may seem obvious, but it is far
from easy to implement. Since 1968 the federal and provincial governments have been engaged in a review of the
constitution. Several times each year the prime ministers
have sat, either before T.V. cameras or in secret, at the
Constitutional Conferences to attempt to hammer out a
new British North America Act.

The difficulties are enormous. Quebec has wanted not
only to prevent federal invasion of so-called provincial
fields, but to have a major voice in such matters of federal
concern as foreign policy and financial policies. The poor
provinces, who benefit from federal equalization payments,
do not want to see the federal government weakened, while
the rich ones are more concerned with their own wealth

Successful operation, but . . .

A comment on the Fulton-Favreau formula, which reflected a wide-spread Canadian concern.

and power. Each premier or prime minister has his eyes on the voter back home, and his political ambitions may at times overshadow his concern for the national interest, or he may assume that what is good for his province must be good for the country. The federal government feels that too much provincial power may undermine national unity, and deprive it of the power to pursue counter-cyclical policies, encourage national development, and assist the poorer provinces.

The last Constitutional Conference at Victoria in June 1971 made a notable breakthrough. The federal government accepted the primary responsibility of the provinces in the field of social welfare, without excluding Ottawa from making payments to individuals. In return Quebec, which had long insisted on provincial control of social welfare, accepted a formula for amending the constitution. Previous attempts to work out a formula for amending the British North America Act, particularly the crucial matter of the division of legislative power, had been wrecked on the shoals of Quebec nationalism.

This was particularly true of the famous Fulton-Favreau formula of 1964. The formula provided that most parts of the B.N.A. Act could be amended with the approval of Ottawa and two-thirds of the provinces with at least 50 per cent of the population. Moreover, any four provinces could delegate some of their power to the federal government if they wished, while Ottawa could in turn delegate its power to the provinces. Although Premier Lesage himself accepted the formula, many in Quebec argued that it would close the door to a further expansion of provincial power and make the achievement of a "special status" for Quebec impossible. Premier Lesage had to back down and the formula was dead.

At Victoria the premiers agreed to a formula whereby the constitution could be amended with the approval of the federal Parliament, every province that has at least 25 per cent of the Canadian population (that is, both Ontario and Quebec), two western provinces, and two Atlantic provinces. The same criticisms that had been levelled at the Fulton-Favreau formula were immediately voiced: particularly that a veto for Quebec would put the constitution in a straightjacket, and that the formula was a further triumph for provincial rights which would ultimately destroy the central government. As this book is going to press, the country is waiting to see whether the provincial governments will accept the formula worked out by their leaders. After the demise of the Fulton-Favreau formula, few people are optimistic.

Who taxes and who spends is, perhaps, not even the most important question Canadian governments face in the 1970's. The incessant battle between the federal and provincial governments for money reflects the fact that since the end of the Second World War—and particularly in the 1960's—government spending has increased at a dramatic rate. In 1952 all governments—federal, provincial and municipal—spent $6.2 billion. By 1960 this figure had jumped to $10.8, and by 1971 the figure had soared to $31.4 billion as Canadians demanded more education, highways, social services, and a host of other benefits from their governments. Governments were hard pressed to secure the necessary revenues, and by 1971 the annual deficit had risen to almost $2 billion. But at the same time as the public wanted more government spending, they had no desire to pay higher taxes. Observing that the country faced higher taxes or increased debts if spending did not level off, the Federal-Provincial Tax Structure Committee declared in 1970:

> But with all levels of government combined requiring upwards of one-third of Canada's total output of goods and services—whether for direct public use or for redistribution among the people of the country— the decisions as to the allocation of those resources and the further relative enlargement of public spending become increasingly critical. Whatever the tests that governments may apply in such decisions—the responsiveness or resistance of taxpayers, the stability and growth of the economy, or the social objectives and aspirations of the voters—the importance of careful analysis and increasing efficiency in the total public sector is clearly highlighted.

The Canadian federal state and the Canadian people, then, face two major questions in the 1970's: Who shall tax and spend? How high shall taxes rise and on what shall the money be spent?

7 QUEBEC AND CANADA

It should not have taken the bombs and murders of the F.L.Q. to underline how impossible it is to understand the contemporary problems of the Canadian state and society without an insight into the mood and aspirations of Quebec. In recent years pressure from Quebec has forced Canadians to rethink the nature of their federal system, and to examine their beliefs about bilingualism and bi-culturalism. The exercise has not been academic, for nothing less is at stake than the survival of the Canadian nation as we know it.

Like most contemporary problems the relations between Quebec and the rest of Canada have a long history. French Canadians have not forgotten that they were conquered by the British two hundred years ago. Their history recalls with pride the Rebellion of 1837, when Louis Joseph Papineau and the Patriotes took up arms to emancipate themselves from British domination—both by the Anglo-Saxons in Quebec and by the British government in London. Their post-Conquest heroes are those who have struggled for the survival of French Canada within an English-speaking nation and continent. *La survivance* has been the motto or rallying cry for two centuries.

To the French Canadians Confederation was less a happy union of the British North American colonies to create a great new nation, than a recognition of the failure of French and English to live harmoniously in the united colony of the Canadas. The federal solution was a compromise between their desire to be a separate people and the historical, geographical, economic and political realities that made this impossible. To them—and to some English Canadians also—Confederation represented a moral compact between two peoples. Canada would be a nation of two cultures, the homeland of two peoples. French and English were recognized as the two Canadian languages,

The teaching of Canadian history and government has not always aided mutual French and English understanding.

and the central government in Ottawa was to protect the guaranteed rights of educational and language minorities—the English in Quebec and the French in other provinces and territories.

Implicit in Confederation was the doctrine of peaceful coexistence, a cultural and political *détente* worked out by the Fathers and sanctioned by an act of the British Parliament. Peaceful coexistence was made possible by the distribution of powers in Sections 91-94 of the B.N.A. Act, which gave to the provincial governments all matters of unique concern to each cultural group. The residual powers of the federal government quite clearly embraced matters that transcended religious, linguistic, or cultural interests. Hopefully, the political arena would thus be free from the storms of cultural conflict and ethnic combat that had paralyzed the united Canadas before 1867. Hitherto dominated by the obsession for *la survivance* in a colony no longer French, *les Canadiens* saw Confederation as an accomplishment that would remove their fears and allow not only survival but growth in a bicultural federal state.

These happy expectations were never realized. The ink was scarcely dry on the British North America Act when the French Canadians realized that Canada was basically an English-speaking country, and that only in Quebec could they remain French. Moving beyond the borders of the province, they encountered an alien and hostile culture, an educational system that denied their children the right to be educated in their own language and faith, and a legal and social structure that denied the equality they felt Confederation had guaranteed. By the turn of the century Henri Bourassa, the brilliant French-Canadian—and Canadian—nationalist, could compare the French to the Indians, who had no rights once they left the reservation.

Confederation, in short, did not bring the two peoples together, inside Quebec or across the country. Within a decade of Confederation Pierre Chaveau, a Quebec Premier, wrote, "English and French, we climb by a double flight of stairs towards the destinies reserved for us on this continent, without knowing each other, without meeting each other, and without even seeing each other, except on the landing of politics." Moreover, the landing of politics had quickly become a battleground on which French Canada came to question the federal system as a satisfactory instrument of government. What had also quickly become clear was that racial and religious questions could not be removed from national politics.

The Riel Rebellions in Manitoba and the Northwest and the execution of Louis Riel in 1885 bitterly divided English and French. The English-Canadian and Protestant opposition to French and Catholic schools outside Quebec revealed how widespread and deepseated was the English-Canadian opposition to a bilingual and bicultural state. To the English, public schools were national schools, the instruments to forge an Anglo-Canadian nationalism. English Canadians also saw Canada as an integral part of the British Empire, and successfully demanded that Canada fight in the Boer War in 1899, despite the strong objections of French Canadians. Again in the First World War,

A 1917 election poster

French Canada could only protest in vain when English Canada demanded compulsory military service.

From each of these crises and these defeats—for every crisis was a defeat—French Canada learned a painful but memorable lesson. National politics could centre on racial, religious and cultural issues. When it did, the minority was powerless, given the democratic philosophy that numbers count. When the nation divided on racial lines, a minority of one was powerless. French Canada could only plead with the majority to be understanding and just. As a result, survival remained the touchstone of political and social action in Quebec. In some French Canadians the dream of a separate state—someday, somehow—had been reawakened.

At the same time, however, the policy of survival was becoming increasingly difficult. Survival had relied in part on isolation from English Canada. In the twentieth century, however, this isolation became increasingly impossible. By 1900 Canada was entering a period of rapid industrialization. Rich forest and mineral resources, abundant supplies of hydro-electric power, the excellent sea-going ports of Quebec and Montreal and a large supply of inexpensive labour led to the growth of industries in Quebec. There was a flood of labour from the farms to the cities, and the old rural isolation was no longer possible. French Canada had become part of the commercial and industrial life of Canada and North America.

The factories and cities represented a threat to survival; they also were breeding grounds for new kinds of English-French hostility. The owners and managers of the new industries were not French Canadians, but American, British and English-Canadian capitalists. Rural French Canada had not built up large amounts of capital for investment, and the government of Quebec encouraged foreign and English-Canadian investment. Moreover, the Quebec educational system run by the Roman Catholic Church had emphasized the classics, religion and the humanities—all guardians of culture—but had not trained people to be technicians, businessmen and scientists.

Thus in their own province the French Canadians became the hewers of wood and the drawers of water in an urban and industrial society dominated by others. By the 1960's French Canadians were the most poorly paid workers within Quebec, earning even less than new immigrants from Europe. Their standard of living was ten per cent lower than that of the average Canadian, and twenty per cent lower than in the neighbouring province of Ontario. Population growth was slowing down as the birth rate fell and some French Canadians emigrated to other provinces where they could earn higher wages.

By the 1950's the province of Quebec was ripe for radical social and economic change. From the universities, from the press, from trade unions came a flood of criticism about the state of affairs in Quebec. Most of the criticism was directed at the provincial government itself. French-Canadian politicians, conservative, wedded to the old ways and values and dominated by the concern for survival, were blamed for selling the province out to foreign capitalists, for following old-fashioned labour policies, for turning their backs on social reform. The Church and the educational system, which the government left largely in the hands of the Church, were blamed for a standard of

"Now here's the plan. We anchor in the St. Lawrence. Darkness. We put ashore. Muffled oars and all that. Scale the cliffs below the Plains of Abraham. Dawn. The bugle sounds . . ." There are Canadians who have expressed views not unlike those of the Colonel Blimps in Victoria, always a favourite target for **Vancouver Sun** cartoonist, Len Norris.

education that did not fit the young French Canadian for playing a full role in modern society.

Gérard Filion, a prominent French Canadian, assessed the problem and assigned responsibility:

> Labour drawn to the cities since the last war came from the countryside and had grade school education, that is, at most Grade 7. These workers landed into a technological civilization without general education and without technical training . . . for the education system we have given ourselves, and for which we are alone responsible, inevitably led to a scorn for economic things and an exaltation of so-called cultural values. It was not the Americans, it was not the English-Canadians, it was not even the English-speaking Quebeckers who inflicted on us for 100 years the education system we had. It is the French Canadian society which gave itself this system, with the consequences we observe today.

Yet English Canadians were not blameless. English was the working language of the new urban and industrial com-

mercial society and French Canadians were handicapped
by having to use their second language in their work.
Business practices and organization reflected the Anglo-
Saxon and not the French mind and character. Large
companies were often too eager to exploit the natural and
human resources of the province, with too little concern for
the welfare of the community.

Discontent mounted during the 1950's. Finally, in 1960
the old politicians of the National Union Party were swept
out by a Liberal Party that had adopted a policy of widespread reform. Social legislation, new labour laws, changes
in the educational system and political reform followed fast
upon the heels of the Liberal victory. Long accustomed to
casting scorn on what they regarded as backward Quebec,
English Canadians were quick to applaud. Their applause
soon became muted, however, when it became clear that
the internal revolution in Quebec would demand great
changes in Canada itself.

No longer content with a form of survival that seemed
no more than a lingering death, French Canadians in
Quebec looked to the future. Deserting their old motto
they now insisted that the future demanded that they be
maîtres chez nous—masters in our own house. This not only
involved regaining control of the economy for French
Canadians—the hydro-electric companies were purchased by
the government in 1962, for example—but also vastly
increasing the powers of the province of Quebec itself
within the Canadian federal system.

Quebec, the French Canadians argued, was not a province like the others. It was, in the cultural sense, a nation
which, like other nations, had its own history, its own
culture, its own resources to be used by its own distinctive
people; and in the provincial government it had its own
institutions. Quebec was not a province; it was *l'état du
Québec*. While the new Liberal government and most
Quebeckers felt that a radically revised federal system could
satisfy their demands, there were some who believed that a
separate state was the only workable solution.

The growth of discontent in Quebec forced a response
by the federal government. While it—and the other
provinces—could not accept all the demands for extended

Pierre Elliott Trudeau is a staunch French-Canadian nationalist, but he is an equally firm believer in Canadian federalism. Before becoming Prime Minister he published a book, which soon afterwards became compulsory reading for Members of Parliament. It was after reading **Federalism and the French Canadians** that Paul Hellyer resigned from the Cabinet, for he realized that Mr. Trudeau and he differed over the federal government's responsibility for housing.

provincial powers and revenues, Prime Minister Pearson in 1963 appointed a Royal Commission on Bilingualism and Biculturalism. Seven years and $7 million later the Commission had finished the last stages of its work. The Commission pointed out with telling documentation the inequalities French Canadians suffered in the civil service, the work world, and schools outside the province. As the Commission worked, the governments of Mr. Pearson and Mr. Trudeau attempted to remedy some of the most obvious inequalities. Civil servants were encouraged to become bilingual, and in 1970 an experiment in French-language work units was started. The provinces were asked to make French an official language or, at least, to serve French-speaking Canadians in French. The federal government provided millions of dollars to support minority language schools across Canada. Businesses in Quebec also made tardy moves to strike at the roots of nationalism and separatism: French Canadians were appointed to senior positions; English-Canadian executives took crash courses in French; and, under pressure from the Quebec government, French increasingly became the language of work.

Yet the pace of constitutional and cultural reform was too slow in Canada and the pace of social reform too slow in Quebec to stop the growth of nationalism and separatism. By 1960 there were several groups in the province that openly advocated the establishment of a separate state. While most favoured a democratic solution to the problem, there were several organizations that advocated violence and revolution. In 1968 the democratic separatists came together under the banner of René Lévesque to form the *Parti Québecois*. Mr. Lévesque had been the most dynamic member of the Lesage Cabinet until its defeat in 1966, but had gradually become convinced not only that separation was the answer, but that Quebec needed much more radical social and economic reforms than those advocated by the Liberals. The combination of his ultra-nationalism, his radical policies, and his personal appeal made the *Parti Québecois*, the *péquistes* as they are called, a formidable political force.

The eyes of the country were on Quebec as the province went to the polls on April 29, 1970. Facing the tottering National Union government were the Liberals under Robert Bourassa, a staunch believer in federalism provided provincial powers and revenues could be expanded, and René Lévesque, who asked the voters to say OUI to a separate state. English Canada was unanimous in its support of the Liberals, and was alarmed by the pre-election polls that revealed *péquiste* strength. Business leaders and federalists predicted economic catastrophe for an independent Quebec, and a fleet of Brinks trucks moved securities from Montreal to Toronto to underline the danger.

The Liberals won the election with 72 seats to the *Parti Québecois'* seven, with the National Union and the *Ralliement des Créditistes* winning 17 and 12 seats respectively. "Today this feels like a splendid country," exclaimed the Toronto *Globe and Mail* the next morning, "for the Province of Quebec is alive and well in Canada." But the Montreal *Star*'s more sober comment that "Quebec has granted us a second chance" was more appropriate. For while the Liberals secured 72 seats they only secured 42 per cent of the popular vote, while René Lévesque had won 23 per cent. Given the fact that English-speaking Quebec had voted solidly Liberal, the strength of separatist feeling among French Canadians was alarming. One study of the election estimated that among French-Canadian voters the Liberals secured 32.6 per cent of the vote and the *Parti Québecois* 28.7. Democratic separatism had become a real possibility in the Canadian state.

More immediately threatening were the activities of the militant separatists. During the 1960's there had been a number of groups in Quebec that had advocated and used violent means to secure a separate state. By 1970 the most important was the *Front de libération du Québec*—the F.L.Q. Since 1963 the F.L.Q. had committed dozens of robberies to secure money, dynamite and arms; planted scores of bombs in mail boxes, private homes, public and private buildings; and been responsible for the deaths of five people and the wounding of many others.

At 8:15 a.m. on October 5, 1970, the F.L.Q. moved one step further when they kidnapped James Cross, the British Trade Commissioner in Montreal. In return for his release they demanded the release of members of the F.L.Q. in jail and their safe passage to Cuba or Algeria, $500,000 in gold, and the publication of an F.L.Q. manifesto. The manifesto, which was read on Radio-Canada as the federal and provincial governments attempted to save the life of Mr. Cross, made it clear that the F.L.Q. was not only, or even mainly, separatist, but was a revolutionary organization. Sections of the manifesto contained the following statements:

> The *Front de libération du Québec* is not a messiah nor a modern-day Robin Hood. It is a group of Quebec workers who have decided to use all means to make sure that the people of Quebec take control of their destiny.
> *The Front de libération du Québec* wants the total independence of all Québecois, united in a free society, purged forever of the clique of voracious sharks, the patronizing "big bosses" and their henchmen who have made Quebec their hunting preserve for "cheap labour" and unscrupulous exploitation. . . .
> We have had our fill of a federal system which

exercises a policy of heavy importation while turning out into the street the low wage earners in the textile and shoe manufacturing trades. . . .

We have had our fill of the hypocrite Bourassa who reinforces himself with Brinks armour, the veritable symbol of the foreign occupation of Quebec, to keep the poor natives of Quebec in the fear of misery and unemployment in which they are accustomed to living. . . .

We have had our fill of promises of jobs and prosperity while we always remain the cowering servants and bootlickers of the big shots who live in Westmount, Town of Mount Royal, Hamstead and Outremont; all the fortresses of high finance on St. James and Wall Streets, while we, the Québecois, have not used all our means, including arms and dynamite, to rid ourselves of these economic and political bosses. . . .

Workers of Quebec, start today to take back what is yours; take for yourselves what belongs to you . . . make your own revolution in your own areas, in your own places of work. . . .

Our struggle can only be victorious. You cannot hold an awakening people indefinitely in misery and contempt. Long live free Quebec.

Long live our comrades who are political prisoners.

Long live the Quebec revolution.

Long live the *Front de libération du Québec.*

Five days after the Cross kidnapping another F.L.Q. cell kidnapped Pierre Laporte, a Quebec cabinet minister. Pressure mounted on the Ottawa and Quebec governments. The majority of Canadians, English and French, favoured a hard line, but a number of leading French Canadians urged the government to free the so-called "political prisoners," that is members of the F.L.Q. who were in jail for robbery and bombing. Radical nationalists and F.L.Q. members and sympathizers attempted to stir up support for the F.L.Q. and by October 14-15 had succeeded in organizing student strikes and demonstrations. Faced with the danger of widespread civil disorder and warned that the police could no longer guarantee to keep order, the Quebec government asked Prime Minister Trudeau to send the army into Quebec on October 15. A day later they

His true colors

Not really, for while all members of the F.L.Q. were separatists, the democratic separatists led by René Lévesque deplored and condemned the tactics of the F.L.Q. Yet there were many English Canadians—and French Canadians—who shared the views of the cartoonists during the tragedy of the October 1970 crisis.

asked him to proclaim the War Measures Act to give the police exceptional powers to seek out the kidnappers. (See Chapter 10.) The Chenier Cell replied by strangling Pierre Laporte.

In the end James Cross was located, and freed by his kidnappers in return for their safe passage to Cuba. The Laporte murderers were caught and brought to trial. Other members of the F.L.Q., which was declared an illegal organization, faced trial for membership in the revolutionary organization or for sedition. By the spring of 1971 the immediate crisis was over. But the problems of separatism and economic and social reform remained. So too did the scars of bitterness and hatred in a nation that had to witness the suspension of civil liberties and the rule of law to deal with a small group of fanatics who preferred the model of Fidel Castro to the slow process of democracy.

It would be a mistake to confuse the terrorists of the F.L.Q. with René Lévesque and the democratic separatists. But it would be equally foolhardy not to understand the aspirations of modern Quebec, and its determination to fight for cultural equality and, both federally and provincially, for rapid economic and social reform. The pace of change in Quebec and Canada may well determine the future relations between English and French Canada and the future of the country.

8 PROVINCIAL AND MUNICIPAL GOVERNMENT

The structure of the ten provincial governments in Canada is almost identical to that of the national government. The provinces have representative and responsible government. Their legislature, Cabinet and Prime Minister serve the same functions and play the same roles as in the national government. But the provincial and federal governments exercise different powers, and in addition the provincial government also delegates some of its authority to local or municipal councils which superintend many of our everyday activities.

The Lieutenant-Governor

The most obvious difference in the structure of the provincial government is that the Lieutenant-Governor, the chief executive officer in the province, who corresponds to the Governor-General, does not represent the Queen directly as does his more distinguished counterpart in Ottawa. The Lieutenant-Governor is appointed by the Governor-General, on the advice of the Prime Minister of Canada, to represent the Crown in the provincial government, to perform such duties as opening and closing the legislature and to give assent to bills that are passed there. But he is also the representative of the federal government; it pays his salary and can dismiss him from office, as it has done on two occasions. For thirty years after Confederation, the Lieutenant-Governors were very active on behalf of the federal government, but as time has passed this activity has virtually ceased. Yet as late as 1937 in Alberta and 1961 in Saskatchewan, Lieutenant-Governors did reserve bills for Ottawa's consideration, a sharp reminder that the powers originally given to them as federal officials still exist and may be used. But on the whole the Lieutenant-Governor is a miniature of the Governor-General.

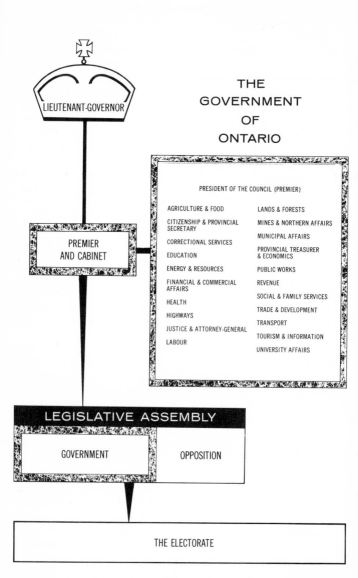

THE
GOVERNMENT
OF
ONTARIO

PRESIDENT OF THE COUNCIL (PREMIER)

AGRICULTURE & FOOD

CITIZENSHIP & PROVINCIAL
SECRETARY

CORRECTIONAL SERVICES

EDUCATION

ENERGY & RESOURCES

FINANCIAL & COMMERCIAL
AFFAIRS

HEALTH

HIGHWAYS

JUSTICE & ATTORNEY-GENERAL

LABOUR

LANDS & FORESTS

MINES & NORTHERN AFFAIRS

MUNICIPAL AFFAIRS

PROVINCIAL TREASURER
& ECONOMICS

PUBLIC WORKS

REVENUE

SOCIAL & FAMILY SERVICES

TRADE & DEVELOPMENT

TRANSPORT

TOURISM & INFORMATION

UNIVERSITY AFFAIRS

LIEUTENANT-GOVERNOR

PREMIER
AND CABINET

LEGISLATIVE ASSEMBLY

GOVERNMENT

OPPOSITION

THE ELECTORATE

Since the provinces have responsible government, the Lieutenant-Governors act on the advice of ministers responsible to the legislature, in other words the Premier and his Cabinet. On occasion Lieutenant-Governors have shown considerable independence, sometimes disregarding the advice of their Cabinets and even refusing a request for a dissolution (as Lord Byng did in 1926 in Ottawa). Several provincial Lieutenant-Governors have dismissed their advisers or forced their resignation for alleged corruption, and one for alleged incompetence.

The Provincial Legislature

There is one major difference between the provincial and federal legislatures. No province has a second chamber corresponding to the Senate. The colonies had appointed Legislative Councils before Confederation. Ontario abolished hers in 1867, and so did British Columbia when she joined Canada. New Brunswick and Prince Edward Island abolished theirs later in the nineteenth century, while Nova Scotia delayed until 1928, largely because of the reluctance of the Legislative Council to pass the necessary legislation to abolish itself. Manitoba was given a Legislative Council in 1870, but the expenses it involved and general agreement that it was not needed led to its abolition in 1876. Quebec did not abolish its Legislative Council until 1968, when it also changed the name of the Legislative Assembly to the National Assembly. There is nothing to suggest that the provinces have suffered without a second chamber.

Otherwise the provincial and federal legislatures are much the same. The same traditions and rules are followed, although the formalities have often been modified in the interests of efficiency. In addition, the smaller house permits a more informal atmosphere than does the larger House of Commons. In the legislature the Premier and his Cabinet exercise the same kind of dominance as do their counterparts in Ottawa. The provincial Cabinet itself, while smaller, represents different regions, religious groups and economic interests within the province. As in Ottawa each minister usually heads a department, although it is much more common for the Premier also to have a department and for one minister to have more than one portfolio.

The departments shown in the chart on page 136, as well as the list in Section 92 of the British North America Act and the discussion on pages 101-5, give an idea of the functions performed by the provincial government. A considerable amount of provincial power is delegated to municipal institutions.

The Nature of Municipal Government

In Canada the basic unit of local government is the municipality. The municipalities possess only the power given to them by the provinces, and are part of the provincial governmental system. As a result, they differ from province to province. In tiny Prince Edward Island, with a population of only about 100,000, they hardly exist, since it is possible to govern the entire province from the provincial capital. But in populous Ontario, which is larger than many nations, municipal governments are imperative and have long been highly developed. In addition, there is a great variety of municipal institutions. Consequently, it is impossible to discuss the organization of municipal government in detail.

A municipality may be either rural or urban. Rural municipalities in the various provinces may be counties, parishes, townships, rural or municipal districts or district municipalities. Urban municipalities are villages, towns and cities. In most Canadian provinces there must be a population of 5,000 to 15,000 before a municipality may achieve the status of a city. As one would expect, in general, the larger the population in a municipality, the greater are the powers delegated to it by the province. Provincial laws outline qualifications for electors and members of municipal bodies. In most cases voters must be Canadian citizens or British subjects and owners or tenants, although in some provinces there is no property qualification.

The growth of large cities has posed a new problem in local government. As a rule such cities as Winnipeg, Vancouver, Toronto and Montreal expand into the neighbouring municipalities until one huge urban area is created. Although the whole metropolitan area thus formed will have similar needs that can only be met by common action, no municipality wishes to give up its separate existence and be absorbed into another. The answer in many Canadian cities has been to form a *metropolitan* government, which is like a miniature federation. Each member of the metropolitan government retains its independent existence and some of its powers, but agrees to be part of a larger organization to which it gives up some of its duties.

However it is not easy to make a metropolitan system work harmoniously and efficiently. Difficulties in Metropolitan Toronto, which was created in 1953, led to the appointment of H. Carl Goldenberg as a one-man Royal Commission to examine the myriad problems posed by the growth of the Megalopolis. Presented to Premier John Robarts in June 1965, the Goldenberg Report recommended that the thirteen municipalities composing Metro Toronto be reorganized into a four-city borough system. Other recommendations included a three-year term of municipal office in place of the existing two-year term, a uniform municipal tax levy for education on a Metro-wide basis, a uniform building by-law and unified traffic engineering and ambulance services.

However, in response to popular pressure, the Ontario government modified the Goldenberg proposals in the interests of increased local autonomy. In April 1966, the government introduced legislation that would reorganize Metro into five boroughs and one city. An enlarged Metro Council of thirty-two members, elected for a three-year term, would be the dominant body in municipal government with borough and city councils playing a relatively minor role. The twenty borough representatives on the Metro Council would for the first time give the suburbs a dominant position over the city. Despite widespread protests, the Metro Chairman would continue to be an appointed, rather than a directly elected, representative of the people.

Critics of the legislation charged that it would not solve the basic weaknesses of division of authority between the central and the local governments and the city-suburban rivalry which has plagued Metro Toronto. The Toronto *Globe and Mail* wrote:

> The schisms within Metro remain, presenting the dismal prospect of parochialism ad nauseam, six different and competing standards of education, squabbling about whether a council should abolish its board of control, and the continued indignity for every voter of having his destiny guided by a Metro chairman appointed to his office without reference to the people he must represent.

For once, the *Toronto Star* agreed with its morning rival.

> Now, after 13 years of experience, was surely the time to take the next logical step and amalgamate the municipalities into a single city.
>
> This would not only have brought about a simpler and more sensible form of government. It would have ensured a common tax rate and a common standard of services for the whole area. It would have stopped the endless bickering between rival governments which has been the bane of Metro, slowing down progress in public housing to a crawl, as one example, and preventing, for another, the creation of a Centennial project worthy of a great city. A single civic government, in the nature of things, would have far greater authority and prestige, would be able to plan and act more boldly in meeting urgent problems, than any "federal" system.

It is probably unnecessary to add that the sentiments of the big city papers were not echoed by many of their weekly suburban counterparts.

The Role of the Municipalities

It is obvious that the problems of municipal government are numerous and complex. Yet it is imperative to find solutions, for the tasks of municipal administration are many, and important to our welfare. For most of us, the water we drink, the schools we attend, the sidewalks we walk on, the roads we drive on, the buses we ride are all provided by the municipality. For some of us in the cities, even the air we breathe is cleaned by municipalities which

MUNICIPAL EXPENDITURES: A COMPARISON

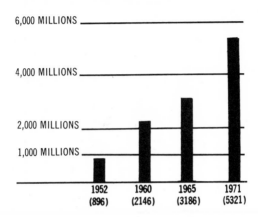

While the chart shows the increasing responsibilities of municipalities, we should also remember some of the increase is due to the decreasing value of the dollar.

pass regulations against air pollution (although the legislation and policing is often ineffective). Health and Welfare services of a wide variety, building control and slum clearance, local court houses and jails, juvenile and family courts, civil defence, sewage, parks and playgrounds, dog tags and pedlars' licences, libraries, electricity and hospitals are more often than not provided or controlled by the municipal authorities. This list is by no means exhaustive, but it should indicate how much of our daily life is affected by the actions or lack of action of the municipal government.

As the provinces assumed more and more responsibilities during this century, they in turn passed many of them on to the municipalities. To a large extent the provinces control the municipalities and supervise their activities through Departments of Municipal Affairs. The chart above shows clearly the increase in municipal expenditures in Canada, the bulk of which is spent on education and public welfare.

"Please don't rock the boat," wrote cartoonist John Collins over his cartoon in the Montreal **Gazette** on January 30, 1970.

To meet this rapidly increasing expenditure, the municipalities have been forced to rely on very limited revenue, much of which comes from property taxes. Yet increased property taxes are felt very directly and keenly by those who have to pay them. As a result, municipal voters are often reluctant to vote even for worthwhile undertakings because they can foresee an immediate increase in their taxes. Moreover, in a new and rapidly expanding municipality, roads and sewers and other facilities have to be installed before a cent has been returned in the form of taxes. This means that the municipalities have to borrow heavily. As more and more ˮduties are laid upon them by the provinces, the municipalities are asking for increased financial support from the provincial governments. In their turn, the provinces complain that they are not receiving enough for their own needs and appeal to the federal government for assistance.

Thus to the dilemma of federal-provincial relations must be added that of federal-provincial-municipal relations. Few people would deny the seriousness of the problem that faces Canada during the next generation. At the very root of it lie the difficulties of municipal governments. One newspaper has commented editorially that local government has had to assume a major part of the costly consequences of industrialization—urban growth, broadened education, millions of cars with their consuming demand for streets, expressways, parking facilities. Yet local government still gets a very low percentage of the total amount of taxes. Its taxing resources are largely the same as when our cities were mainly market towns. Closely related as it is to the constitutional problem of federal-provincial relations, the municipal problem will not be easy to solve. The great danger is that Canada may succumb to the paralyzing rigidity of a constitutional straightjacket that is a survival from the days when our country was truly a nation of country villages and market towns.

9 THE MEN BEHIND THE LINES

The Civil Service

For every soldier in the front line there are, we are told, ten behind the line, and for every pilot in the air, ten airmen on the ground. Government also has its men behind the lines. The federal government alone has over three hundred thousand employees, known as civil servants, or public servants. If the employees of the provincial and municipal governments were added to this number, the figure would approach half a million. This means that at least one out of every fifty Canadians works for the government at some level. The growth in the *bureaucracy* (a word which means literally "men working at desks"), which is mainly due to the immense expansion of government activities in this century, raises three very important questions: How do we staff our civil services? What are their tasks and how well do they do them? To what extent do we rely on them?

Recruiting

Throughout the nineteenth century in Canada, recruits for the civil service were appointed on the time-honoured principle that "to the victors belong the spoils." Thus the victors in an election usually dismissed many of the civil servants who were then in office and replaced them with their own political friends. Few people seriously believed that this made a good civil service, but some did contend that it was a democratic method of recruiting government employees. One of the most eloquent supporters of the spoils system was President Andrew Jackson of the United States. "The duties of all public offices," said Jackson, "are so plain and simple that men of intelligence may readily qualify themselves for their performance, and I cannot but believe that more is lost by the long continuance of men in office than is generally to be gained by their experience. . . . In a country where offices are created solely for the benefit of the people, no one man has any more intrinsic right to official station than another." Canadians did not openly endorse these ideas—but they often acted on them just the same.

The most common justification of this means of choosing civil servants was that a political party was oiled by such patronage, and that without the oil the party machine would not only squeak but in time would cease to function altogether. As late as 1904 in the Canadian House of Commons, a cabinet minister declared, "As I understand it, the party system prevails in Canada, and it is the practice of the Government of today to remember their supporters in distributing public patronage. That practice has obtained in days gone by and I hope it is in full force today."

By 1904, however, there was a growing movement for civil service reform in Canada. Years before, Great Britain had reformed her civil service by placing entrance and promotions on a basis of competitive merit. Although the Canadian government had flirted with reforms from time to time, political considerations had always stood in the way of action. In 1918, however, the government established a Civil Service Commission to control entrance, promotions and classification of civil servants. The Commission was to be independent of politics and the government.

Yet the spoils system was slow in dying and, indeed, is still far from dead. Today less than half the public servants come within the jurisdiction of the Civil Service Commission. As a result, members of both the federal and provincial legislatures constantly receive requests for positions and in some cases, no doubt, use their influence on behalf of the petitioner. Moreover, though the provinces generally tended to follow the lead of the federal government, in some provinces patronage is far more widespread than on the federal level. Nonetheless, the principle of an independent civil service, with entrance based on standards, and promotions on merit, is firmly established in Canada.

The second question—How well do our civil servants perform their tasks?—is directly related to the method of their appointment. Competitive entrance examinations and promotion on merit have led generally to the creation of a first-class civil service. Members have often been recruited from outside the service, particularly from the universities, to fill high posts. This practice has resulted in a civil service recognized even in other countries as among the best in the world. Some, indeed, claim that it is second to none.

Are We Governed by the Civil Servants?

In answering our third question—How reliant are we on our civil service?—we are not concerned with the typists and clerks, important as they are to the service, but with the experts of the service, the men in research, in diplomacy, in public finance. The higher positions in every department are staffed by men of very specialized education, who have spent years mastering the intricacies of their subjects. Whatever party is in office, these men remain and provide continuity in the service. A new cabinet minister may have ideas, but he usually lacks an intimate knowledge of the affairs of his department. He must depend upon the expert advice given him by the permanent public servants. From time to time, this dependence has aroused the cry that, in fact, we are governed by the civil servants.

In May 1971 Paul Hellyer resigned from the Liberal Party to sit in the Commons as an independent and to start a new political movement called Action Canada. Mr. Hellyer had been a Member of the Commons since 1949 and had been in the Cabinets of Prime Ministers Pearson and Trudeau. In announcing his departure from the Liberal Party, Mr. Hellyer declared, "You might say I'm at war with the system—the way it operates, the way it has operated in the last two Governments." The "system" involved party loyalty and the power of the Prime Minister and a small group of cabinet ministers. But, he added, it also included the civil servants: "A handful of people—a small coterie of a dozen to fifteen top civil servants—make too many decisions. . . . Their views are rubber-stamped down the line by the Cabinet. . . ."

Government, indeed, has become so complex that we cannot get along without the highly skilled experts. This situation raises problems. A century ago a conscientious citizen by following public affairs could, if he wished, reach intelligent conclusions on government matters. The problems with which governments dealt were not beyond the reach of his training and his mind. Today, in a sense, this is no longer true. Questions of economic and financial policy—whether there should be more money in circulation or less, and whether unemployment in the long run is less damaging than inflation—are matters upon which even the experts disagree. Well educated and intelligent as a citizen may be, he often finds that he simply cannot fathom the intricacies of the subject. He then has no alternative but to admit his inability and to side with his favourite party, leader or newspaper. Such a situation is unhealthy, for it may well be that election issues turn on very complex matters. And elections can hardly be purposeful or make much sense if the electorate cannot understand the issues involved.

The experts in the civil service, of course, function only as advisers to the cabinet ministers in charge of the departments. When a cabinet minister has been in office a long time, there will inevitably be a growing confidence between him and the men who counsel him. Consequently, a new minister, representing a different political party, may feel that he cannot rely on the loyalty of his advisers. He may well ask how they could carry out the former government's policy—in part their own policy—and then overnight execute the new government's policy which may be in conflict with the old. Sometimes it happens that the minister is pledged to a policy which the expert thinks is impossible or inadvisable to carry out. In such a case, the expert can offer his opinion, and, whether or not his advice is taken, can then do his best to implement the minister's policy. However, if a serious question of principle is involved, and both the minister and the expert find the situation intolerable, then the latter resigns.

On the whole, the Canadian civil service has measured up to its task as a reasonably impartial, able and honest group of administrators. We must ensure that this continues to be the case. As government activities expand and become more complex, the civil service will continue to grow. The expert civil servant will inevitably become more and more essential to the adequate functioning of Canadian governments on all levels.

10 THE RULE OF LAW AND CIVIL LIBERTY

It is often thought that the police represent the law. It would be more accurate to say that they represent the force behind it. The law itself is made by the legislature and is interpreted and applied in the courts by lawyers and judges who have extensive legal training. Although police forces maintain law and order, it is through our elaborate system of courts that the rule of law is upheld.

In our society the rule of law means something more fundamental than the establishment of common principles to ensure peace and order. Inherent in it is the idea that the law is supreme over any individual or group of individuals.

Law and the Courts

In its simplest sense, law in a democracy is the set of rules and regulations which the people, through their representatives, have agreed upon to make possible an ordered life. Every law restricts and at the same time protects the freedom of the individual in some way. Speed limits restrict the rate at which everyone may drive so that all may drive in safety. If there were no limits set, irresponsible persons would be free to drive at excessive speeds to the danger of all. Business firms are prevented by law from engaging in practices harmful to the public, such as fixing prices or selling impure foods (although the law is often evaded). Such laws are made by the Parliament of Canada, the provincial legislatures or local authorities exercising a general authority granted to them by the provincial governments.

Broadly speaking, there are two kinds of law, criminal law and civil law. Criminal law is concerned with the definition and punishment of such offences as murder, arson and theft. Although these crimes may be committed against individuals they are considered to be crimes against

THE CANADIAN COURT SYSTEM
(AS IT EXISTS IN ONTARIO)

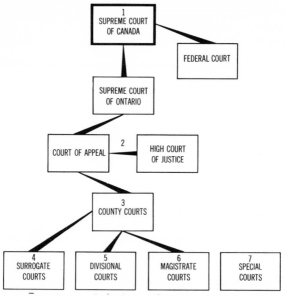

1. The Supreme Court of Canada is the court of final appeal. The decision rests with the Chief Justice and eight judges. The Court hears cases from the provincial courts and the Federal Court. Both criminal cases and civil cases involving over $2,000 can be heard. The Court is sometimes asked by the government for legal advice.

2. The High Court of Justice of Ontario hears mainly original cases of major importance. The Court of Appeal hears appeals from lower courts and the High Court in civil and criminal cases. In criminal cases, the accused may elect trial by jury or by judge alone. In some provinces, the two divisions are combined.

3. In the County Courts, the verdict is reached sometimes by means of a jury trial, sometimes by the judge alone.

4. The Surrogate Courts settle the estates of the dead.

5. Divisional Courts deal with civil cases involving moderate amounts of money, and with minor criminal offences.

6. Magistrate Courts provide redress for minor civil cases. The decision is made by a presiding judge.

7. Juvenile Courts and Family Courts fill a special need in the Canadian court system.

Arrows indicate possible course of a case.

the community as a whole. As a result, the government assumes the responsibility for bringing the criminal to trial. It is not the responsibility of the murdered man's family to seek out the suspected criminal and prosecute him in court. Criminal law, which is the same throughout Canada, is the responsibility of the federal government.

Civil law is concerned with property and civil rights. Such matters as business practices and financial transactions are part of the civil law. Authority over civil law is shared by the provincial and federal governments. Although control over property and civil rights is one of the powers given to the provinces, such matters as banking are under federal jurisdiction. Thus, while there is some uniformity in civil law throughout Canada, there are also differences from province to province. Quebec makes the system more complex because she has retained her own Civil Code, which has a French origin, rather than adopt the laws of Britain which form the basis of the civil law in the other provinces. In civil cases, it is generally the responsibility of the aggrieved person to bring his case into court. One exception to this rule is the case of traffic laws. Although violations of traffic regulations come under the broad category of civil law, they are regarded as offences against the state, and those accused are prosecuted by provincial or municipal authorities.

The Courts

The court system in Canada illustrates again the strong centralizing tendency of our constitution. In the American federation there are two court systems, a federal and a state, with little contact between the two. But in Canada there is really one pyramid of courts. The chart on page 150 shows the general structure of the Canadian court system. Only a few additional comments are necessary. The Federal Court was called the Exchequer Court before 1970 and heard original cases dealing only with financial matters involving the federal government. After 1970 the new court was also charged with hearing appeals from federal administrative boards and tribunals, from which there was no appeal previously. Appeals resulting from the Federal

Court's decisions may be made to the Supreme Court. The Judicial Committee of the Privy Council is not shown because it no longer plays a part in the Canadian judicial system. At one time, it was Canada's final court of appeal in criminal as well as civil and constitutional cases. As we have seen, its decisions had a great effect on the constitutional development of Canada. However, appeals to the Judicial Committee have now been abolished, in criminal cases in 1933, and in all other cases in 1949.

Since the rule of law is the very foundation of free government, our courts are of tremendous importance. The law as interpreted by the courts must have the respect of all. Judges must be men of the highest quality, not only learned but also completely independent and impartial. Although the provincial governments were given the right to organize courts and administer justice within the provinces, the federal government was given the authority to appoint the judges. This was done to give the federal government some control over the administration of justice and also to try to ensure the best and most independent judiciary. (It was felt that if the judges were elected, as many American state judges are, their decisions might be influenced by the need to win votes in the next election.) However, there are problems involved in the appointment of judges in Canada. Since they are appointed by the Governor-General in Council, that is, by the Prime Minister and government of the day, political considerations cannot help but be a factor in their choice. To guard against the obvious danger of political influence, it was decided that judges could be removed only with the consent of both Houses of Parliament. It is unlikely that any government would openly attempt to dismiss a judge in full view of Parliament and the people, other than for gross incompetency or neglect of duty. In most instances judges must retire at the age of 75.

Canadians have good reason to be proud of their judiciary. On the whole, our judges have performed their duties ably and impartially. Unfortunately, there have been a few exceptions. Some judges in the past were notorious political partisans and even left the judicial bench to resume their political activities. A. R. Angers of Quebec, for example, was a provincial cabinet member, Member of Parliament, judge, Lieutenant-Governor, Senator and federal cabinet minister in turn. When he resigned from the Cabinet in 1895, he was offered, but refused, another judgeship. Alexander Morris of Ontario was an active politician before being appointed Chief Justice and then Lieutenant-Governor of Manitoba. When his term as Lieutenant-Governor expired, he returned to active politics in Ontario. Many other examples of party adherents in the judiciary could be cited. It has been argued that to appoint as judges men who have been very active in politics does not encourage the public to regard the judiciary as completely impartial. Even though the judges do forget their political past, many people do not.

Political leaders constantly face strong pressures to grant favours to their friends and supporters. It is the duty of the citizen to act as a watchdog and make it harder for the politicians to make ill-advised appointments, especially in the judiciary.

The Police Force

Our enjoyment of the rule of law depends partly on the nature and calibre of our police forces. In a democracy the police are servants of the people. They are charged with the enforcement of those laws and regulations which the people, through their freely elected representatives, deem necessary for the maintenance of order and security within the country. They are not, as in totalitarian countries, the armed tool by means of which the ruling authorities impose their will on the people. In a democracy the police act on the people's behalf.

In Canada there are several kinds of police force, the most important of which are the federal, provincial and municipal police. The federal police, the famous Royal Canadian Mounted Police, are responsible for the enforcement of all federal laws everywhere in Canada. By special arrangement, they also police eight of the provinces and many municipalities across Canada. Ontario and Quebec have their own provincial police forces which are responsible for law enforcement within their own borders except in those areas that are served by municipal police. Municipal police include county, township and city police forces. They range in size from several thousand policemen in cities like Toronto to one constable in a small village, and are empowered by the provinces to enforce their own municipal and criminal laws.

Many people think of the police in terms of the officers who direct traffic or "pound the beat." Actually, a modern police force is a complex organization of highly trained and well equipped men and women who carry out a wide variety of duties. Members of the Royal Canadian Mounted Police not only investigate every type of crime from safecracking to espionage, but also inspect fisheries, collect taxes in some remote areas and help take the census.

The police perform their difficult, dangerous and often thankless tasks creditably, but there have been occasions when they have abused their authority. No doubt violent and hardened criminals cannot be treated gently, but Professor F. R. Scott of McGill University, a dedicated fighter for civil liberties, cites a number of disturbing instances where the police have exceeded their authority. Among these was the case of a Miss Lamb who "was illegally arrested, held over the weekend in the cells without any charge being laid against her, not allowed to telephone a lawyer and then offered her freedom on condition she sign a document releasing the police from all responsibility for the way they had treated her." One cannot help but wonder with Professor Scott "how many other innocent victims have been similarly treated by the police but have not had the courage and the backing to pursue the matter through to final victory—in this case twelve and one-half years after the arrest had taken place." Fortunately, there is little reason to believe that such examples are common, but there are too many to be accepted in a society governed by the rule of law. In the case of Miss Lamb the courts finally decided that the police had acted illegally, and the guilty officials were forced to pay damages.

Such cases reveal why the public are reluctant to see an extension of police power. An excellent illustration of that

"They don't see it our way, Fred" was the caption **Toronto Star** cartoonist Duncan Macpherson placed under the above cartoon. The tone of the cartoon, and the description of the bill as the Police State Bill, were typical of the reaction of the press and public to the proposed legislation. "Fred" was the Hon. F. M. Cass, the Attorney-General. **The Globe and Mail** referred to the "Bill of Wrongs," while the **Toronto Telegram** made pointed references to the Star Chamber; both were alluding to aspects of the long struggle for the due process of law and civil liberties in England.

reluctance was provided in Ontario in 1964. In an effort to uncover and control organized crime in the province, the government introduced a bill to give extended powers to the Police Commission. The most offensive section of the bill declared that "Where a person . . . (a) refuses to be sworn; (b) having been sworn, refuses to answer the questions that are put to him; (c) refuses to produce any writings that he is required to produce . . . the Commission may, by warrant, commit the person to prison for a period not exceeding eight clear days." If the person still refused to co-operate he could be returned to prison for another eight days—and on and on, until the witness became co-operative. Questioned by reporters, the Attorney-General was reported to have admitted that the bill interfered with individual rights and liberty, but added that "unless the Police Commission takes drastic action, any investigation [of organized crime] will be as abortive as previous ones. . . . The rights of a few individuals may have to be over-ridden for the public good."

The Toronto press, which had been demanding action against organized crime, was not prepared to accept this dismissal of individual liberties and interference with the legal rights of the citizen. So great was the furor in the press and in the legislature that the Premier promised to withdraw the offensive clause, and soon after announced the resignation of the Attorney-General. The case not only demonstrated the public concern for basic rights and free-doms, but also showed how important a free and vigilant press and the opposition in the legislature can be.

This discussion of law and the courts and law-enforce-ment agents leads directly to a discussion of civil liberties or basic freedoms. The very foundation of these freedoms and rights is what is known as the due process of law or the judicial rights of the citizen.

Bill of Rights

Even though our representatives in Parliament can change the law, the conviction persists that there are things which even they cannot change. Our society firmly believes that each individual possesses certain basic freedoms which the government cannot infringe and must, in fact, guaran-tee. These may be listed as freedom of speech, freedom of movement, freedom to worship, freedom of association and assembly, freedom of political choice, freedom to vote, freedom from discrimination on grounds of race or religion or colour, and underlying all these, the right to enjoy the full protection of the law. In Ontario, for ex-ample, the Fair Employment Practices Act makes it illegal for any employer even to inquire as to an applicant's race, creed, colour, nationality or ancestry. Another Act states that hotels, restaurants, stores and so on must not deny service on these grounds. As we all know, however, many people still practise such discrimination, realizing perhaps that few people will file a complaint with the Ontario Anti-Discrimination Commission in Toronto or similar agencies in other provinces. To these basic rights there is a growing insistence in the modern age that we must add freedom from want and insecurity, the right to employment, health, education and leisure.

In many countries, many basic rights are written into the constitution. This was not the case in Canada until the spring of 1960, when a civil rights bill was introduced into the Canadian Parliament where it was fiercely debated. On August 4, after several amendments had been made, it was passed by the House of Commons and on August 10 Governor-General Vanier gave Royal Assent to it and it became law. Previous to this, the majority of people had taken our basic freedoms for granted. Such rights, however, are often violated whether they are written into the constitution or not.

Critics of the Bill point out that it is merely an instruction to judges on how to interpret federal laws. No machinery is created for its enforcement. Furthermore, it does not affect the powers of the provinces, which, in the past, have been the worst violators of human rights. Finally, the rights are applicable only in peacetime. At the same time, however, the Bill is supported by many Canadians who believe that it will be valuable as a statement of basic principles. Professor F. R. Scott, speaking about the Bill, pointed out that ". . . the importance of Magna Carta in the history of England is not diminished by the fact that it could be set aside at any time by any later act of Parliament."

During the discussions of constitutional reform since 1968 Prime Minister Trudeau has attempted to persuade the provinces that a Bill of Rights should become part of a new constitution. At the Victoria Constitutional Conference in June 1971 the premiers agreed that Article I of a new constitution should read:

It is hereby recognized and declared that in Canada every person has the following fundamental freedoms: Freedom of thought, conscience and religion, freedom

Preamble:

The Parliament of Canada, affirming that the Canadian nation is founded upon principles that acknowledge the supremacy of God, the dignity and worth of the human person and the position of the family in a society of free men and free institutions;

Affirming also that men and institutions remain free only when freedom is founded upon respect for moral and spiritual values and the rule of law;

And being desirous of enshrining these principles and the human rights and fundamental freedoms derived from them, in a bill of rights which shall reflect the respect of Parliament for its constitutional authority and which shall ensure the protection of these rights and freedoms in Canada:

Therefore Her Majesty, by and with the advice and consent of the Senate and House of Commons of Canada, enacts as follows:

PART I
Bill of Rights

1. It is hereby recognized and declared that in Canada there have existed and shall continue to exist without discrimination by reason of race, national origin, colour, religion or sex, the following human rights and fundamental freedoms, namely,

(A) The right of the individual to life, liberty, security of the person and enjoyment of property, and the right not to be deprived thereof, except by due process of law;

(B) The right of the individual to equality before the law and the protection of the law;

(C) Freedom of religion;

(D) Freedom of speech;

(E) Freedom of assembly and association; and

(F) Freedom of the press.

BILL OF RIGHTS

PART II

2. . . . no law of Canada shall be construed or applied so as to

(A) Authorize or effect the arbitrary detention, imprisonment or exile of any person;

(B) Impose or authorize the imposition of cruel and unusual punishment;

(C) Deprive a person who has been arrested or detained

(i) Of the right to be informed promptly of the reason for his arrest or detention,

(ii) Of the right to retain and instruct counsel without delay, or

(iii) Of the remedy by way of habeas corpus for the determination of the validity of his detention and for his release if the detention is not lawful;

(D) Authorize a court, tribunal, commission, board or other authority to compel a person to give evidence if he is denied counsel, protection against self-incrimination or other constitutional safeguards;

(E) Deprive a person of the right to a fair hearing in accordance with the principles of fundamental justice for the determination of his rights and obligations;

(F) Deprive a person charged with a criminal offence of the right to be presumed innocent until proved guilty according to law in a fair and public hearing by an independent and impartial tribunal, or of the right to reasonable bail without just cause; or

(G) Deprive a person of the right to the assistance of an interpreter in any proceedings in which he is involved or in which he is a party or a witness, before a court, commission, board or other tribunal, if he does not understand or speak the language in which such proceedings are conducted.

of opinion and expression, and freedom of peaceful assembly and association; and all laws shall be construed and applied so as not to abrogate or abridge any such freedom.

However, read Article III, limitations on such freedoms could be imposed for reasons of "Public safety, order, health or morals, of national security, or of the rights and freedoms of others. . . ."

Due Process of Law

The most important right, now guaranteed in written form in the 1960 Bill of Rights, is the enjoyment of the due process of law. This means primarily that we have freedom from arbitrary or unwarranted arrest and the right to a fair trial. The police must always inform a person of the reason for his arrest. The accused has the right to legal assistance and in most cases is allowed to have bail. If he cannot secure a lawyer, the court may appoint one to defend him. He must be brought to trial within a reasonable period of time. In most cases, an accused person can elect to be tried either by judge or by a judge and jury. Prospective members of a jury may be challenged on the grounds that they are biased, for no one who is prejudiced against the accused is permitted to serve. During a trial, strict rules govern the admissibility of evidence. For example, confessions secured by force or intimidation are not admitted. The entire proceedings are based on the fundamental assumption that every man must be presumed innocent until proven guilty. The view is accepted that it is less serious for a guilty man to go free than for an innocent man to be unjustly punished.

In wartime, there is very little the federal government cannot do in regulating our daily life and imposing serious restrictions on a wide variety of civil liberties. Opinion is divided on the extent to which a government may go in this direction. Although some argue that all rights must be suspended during a war, others maintain that even in wartime there must be some limit to the government's authority. During the Second World War, government in Canada was carried on largely by Orders in Council which were free from normal investigation in Parliament and which could be kept secret. In September 1939, the Defence of Canada Regulations were established by an Order in Council. This measure, designed to meet the wartime emergency, radically curtailed civil rights. Under the Regulations, the Governor in Council (that is, the Cabinet) was given the power to register, arrest, intern or relocate enemy aliens; to take measures against sabotage; to control the movement of people; to requisition and destroy property; to censor telegraphic or postal communications; to prohibit the issuance of any statement, whether true or not, deemed to be harmful to the common cause; to outlaw certain societies detrimental to the national interest; to authorize police or military officers to enter any premises or stop and search any person or vehicle without warrant. From these regulations it may easily be seen that if the men in power had wanted to act as despots nothing could have prevented them from doing so.

Since the war there have been several serious infringements of civil liberties. Two, in a way, were legacies of the war. Through a secret Order in Council, the government assumed large powers to question and detain, on its own authority and under any circumstances, anyone suspected of being a spy. In 1945, following disclosures by Igor Gouzenko, a Russian cipher clerk, of Communist espionage activities in Canada, the government made widespread arrests. Suspects were questioned and detained without due process of law. Although few Canadians questioned the aim of the investigation, which uncovered a Soviet spy ring in Canada, believers in civil liberties deplored the means by which this was accomplished.

Far less justified, however, was the treatment of Canadian citizens of Japanese origin. In 1941, there were thousands of people of Japanese origin living on the west coast of Canada. Over 17,000 were Canadian citizens. When war with Japan broke out in December 1941, the federal government, fearful of spies among the Japanese Canadians, seized fishing vessels, interned suspects and closed Japanese schools. By February 1942 public pressure and government anxiety led to a decision to treat all Japanese Canadians as aliens and to remove them to a distance of more than one hundred miles from the west coast. The Japanese, forced to sell their homes, cars and businesses for what little they could get for them, suffered tremendous losses. Although some were allowed to move to eastern Canada, great numbers were put in road camps and rehabilitated ghost towns. In wartime, when there is an obvious danger of espionage, such actions are understandable. But after the war, the Canadian government continued to curtail the basic freedoms of Japanese Canadians. By Order in Council it assumed the authority to examine the loyalty of Japanese Canadians, deport them to Japan if they were considered undesirable and revoke the Canadian citizenship of such deported persons. Both the Supreme Court and the Judicial Committee of the Privy Council upheld the validity of the Orders.

Many Canadians felt that the treatment of the Japanese was reprehensible. War was one thing; but to allow hatred and passion to survive and dictate policy after the war seemed intolerable. In 1947, the Canadian government repealed the Orders in Council, doubtless with a feeling that injustice had been done.

In 1965-66 in the security investigations centring around Gerda Munsinger, a German immigrant of dubious background and reputation, and around Victor Spencer, a Vancouver postal clerk, the nation was shocked to discover the extent to which private activities might be scrutinized. Revelations that the R.C.M.P. had resorted to wire-tapping and secret photography convinced some citizens that if national security required the infringement of individual rights, the price might be too high. The increasing evidence of widespread industrial espionage, wire-tapping, and eavesdropping, using the whole panoply of twentieth-century technology, raised the spectre that the regulated, dehumanized society envisaged by George Orwell for 1984 had arrived about two decades early.

A more recent, but different, illustration of the infringement of civil liberties was provided in October 1970 when the federal government invoked the War Measures Act in an attempt to curb civil disorder in Quebec and capture the

F.L.Q. kidnappers. Although the vast majority of Canadians approved of the action, few were happy about the curtailment of civil liberties and the suspension of the due process of law it involved. The War Measures Act made membership in the F.L.Q. a crime, when it had not been a crime before; it permitted police to arrest without a warrant; and allowed people to be detained in jail without bail for up to three weeks without a charge being laid. The government defended its action on the grounds that the threat to civil liberties by the F.L.Q. was greater than that posed by the War Measures Act, but the action came under sharp condemnation from many civil rights leaders. While two young Toronto lawyers attacked Prime Minister Trudeau for establishing a "police state," Frank Scott observed "that if they use the power carefully and without abuse—which I think they intend to do—I do not think we have to fear what they do to civil liberties as greatly as that threatened by the F.L.Q." But it was a tragic situation that no Canadian relished, and provided a sharp illustration of the fragility of civil liberties in times of unrest and violence.

Freedom of Speech, Press and Worship

Every person and every newspaper in Canada has the right to express opinions on all public matters. This freedom is essential for the satisfactory working of democratic government. Without it, democracy would be a farce. Like any other freedom, this one has its limits. No person may infringe on the freedom of another or on the welfare of society. Libel, slander and incitement to rebellion are punishable in the courts as crimes against individuals or the state. But people may express any political opinion openly without fear of arrest as long as they do not incite rebellion. Similarly, no restrictions may be placed on a person's religious views. Neighbours may be intolerant and exercise social pressure against members of a religious faith, but the law guarantees freedom of worship to everyone. (Recently, however, the courts have authorized blood transfusions to children of Jehovah's Witnesses despite the religious convictions of the parents, an illustration of the conflict between individual freedom and the common well-being.)

Without these freedoms, life as we wish to live it would be impossible. Countries like Canada, which have inherited the British tradition of law and liberty, have rejected for centuries systems of government that deny freedom of speech, political opinion and worship. Yet we can never afford to take these freedoms for granted. Even in Canada governments have, from time to time, seriously infringed these rights, Over thirty years ago, the Alberta government introduced a bill which would have seriously restricted the freedom of the press. The Lieutenant-Governor refused to give his assent and reserved the bill for the consideration of the federal government which did not approve it.

About the same time, the Quebec government passed the infamous act which became known as the "Padlock Law." This law was supposedly aimed at preventing the spread of Communism and the printing of Communist literature. The Attorney-General of the province was given the authority, upon evidence that satisfied him and without any court action, to close or padlock any premises suspected of being used to spread the doctrines of Communism. Communism was not defined; due process of law was denied in favour of suspicion and hearsay evidence; and the police were given the authority to enter homes, search libraries and seize any literature found. Police even invaded private meetings at McGill University to make note of "dangerous

Soon after the victory of Social Credit in Alberta in 1935 Premier Aberhart began to be annoyed at the criticism of his government and its policies coming from the Alberta press. By June 3, 1936 (when the top cartoon by Arch Dale appeared), he was urging that the press be licensed as "the only way to make them tell the truth." A year later, with the press continuing its sharp criticism of his government, he declared that some control of the press was essential, and had his legislature pass The Accurate News and Information Act which gave the government substantial control over the press. Dale once again, this time far more seriously, hit out at Premier Aberhart. In Toronto, **The Globe and Mail** thundered editorially that "there was nothing in the way of press control, outside the Fascist and Communist countries, that is comparable with it in suppression of freedom of personal liberty."

thoughts." The danger of Communism should not obscure the main significance of the "Padlock Law"—that it gave the provincial government an arbitrary power which infringed basic liberties and that it was a denial of due process of law. A member of the Canadian Bar Association reported in 1937 that "possibly it is under such laws as this that in other lands the homes of respectable and law-abiding citizens are ransacked simply because their owners do not wear a brown or a black shirt."

The religious sect known as Jehovah's Witnesses has also been harried in Quebec, as a result of by-laws made under provincial authority, which prohibited the distribution of any book, pamphlet or circular on the streets without the permission of the Chief of Police. Technically this list could include newspapers, and the by-laws had the effect of placing freedom of the press under police censorship.

The whole question of freedom of expression involves much more than freedom of speech, press and worship. People express themselves, often most creatively, through art, music, literature and the dance. To what extent should freedom of expression through these media be limited? What constitutes the welfare of society? A case in this connection attracted nation-wide attention in May 1965, when Toronto police raided Dorothy Cameron's art gallery and charged her with showing obscene pictures. Subsequently, Miss Cameron was convicted and fined $50 on each of seven counts.

The case attracted the attention of the Canadian Civil Liberties Association. Formed in 1965 "to maintain, defend, and extend fundamental human rights and civil liberties traditional in our society," the Association adopted the statement opposite.

The Association believed that in reaching his decision in the Cameron case the magistrate erred in a number of respects. They said, for example, that he "disregarded the evidence that the apparent theme of the pictures has long been accepted as a legitimate subject of art and that in portraying the theme the artists produced serious and honest works having genuine artistic merit." In addition, he "overlooked the fact that the community will accept a

CANADIAN CIVIL LIBERTIES ASSOCIATION

We believe

. . . That the freedom of all men is diminished when the rights of one man are denied.

. . . That in a Democratic Society each person has the responsibility to defend the right of every other person. . . .

- • To speak in public and express his ideas both critical and otherwise, without restriction, no matter how unpopular his ideas may be.
- • To be governed by his conscience in matters of belief.
- • To participate fully in the community in work, accommodation, and recreation, regardless of his race, religion, colour, sex, or national origin.
- • To choose what books he will read and what art, drama, and entertainment he will enjoy, without restrictions or pre-censorship.
- • To privacy and from unreasonable interference with his home, person, or reputation.
- • To enjoy a free press.
- • To associate freely with others, both privately and publicly, and to demonstrate peacefully.
- • To protest and take action to reform unjust or outmoded laws which infringe upon his civil liberties.
- • To attend public educational institutions where ideas are presented fully and may be debated without restrictions or taboos.
- • To be treated with respect by police and other law enforcement agents.
- • To immediate judicial consideration of the legality of his detention.
- • To a fair public trial, to protection against undue delay, self-incrimination, to the assistance of counsel and an opportunity to make a full defence.*

*This statement is reproduced by permission of the Canadian Civil Liberties Association.

graphic artistic portrayal by writers, artists, opera composers, and ballet choreographers of activities which the community highly disapproves." Not only did the magistrate fail to

evaluate the evidence of the experts that "the exhibition
made a highly significant contribution to Canadian art,"
but he "completely failed to consider the irreparable harm
which will flow from the banning of the art. The reper-
cussions which would result from proscribing and inhibit-
ing the creative instincts of artists, by curtailing the freedom
of artists to disseminate the concept of their imaginations,
are without measure. If the reasoning of the Magistrate is
upheld, members of your community may for years be
denied the right to view the originals or reproductions of
the works of many of the Masters, past, present and future.
It could well prevent art galleries, museums, libraries, universities and other similar institutions from exhibiting
works generally regarded as a legitimate portion of the
cultural heritage of the civilized world."

All of the cases mentioned indicate how dangerous it is
for the citizens, even of a country like Canada, to assume
that civil liberties and human rights may be threatened only
in countries with authoritarian governments. The defence
of civil liberties cannot be left to any one person or institution, whether Parliament, or the court, or the legal
profession. It must be defended by the public as a whole.
As U.S. Vice-President Hubert Humphrey pointed out,
"Freedom is a fragile thing. Too many nations have dis-
covered that to become free is not enough. You have to
work at keeping free." This conviction that freedom is
everybody's business has led to the formation of many
voluntary civil liberties associations like the C.C.L.A. in
several of the larger Canadian cities. These associations
have helped to promote fair employment laws, the Human
Rights Code and ultimately the Canadian Bill of Rights.
The Bill is a healthy indication that Canadians are becoming more concerned about civil liberties. As we look more
and more to government for a wide variety of services, we
create more and more bodies with authority over us. More
and more people have the opportunity and power to violate
our freedoms. As citizens, we should never forget that the
power of public officials is also limited by law, and that
even the Prime Minister of Canada can be sued for exceeding his authority.

11 BRITISH AND AMERICAN COMPARISONS

From time to time we have used the British or American systems of government as a model to show how the Canadian system took shape. In such a short study as this, it would be impossible to discuss the workings of these other systems in any detail; but it might be fruitful to point out some of the major comparisons and contrasts in order to throw the Canadian system into sharper focus, and to enable us better to understand the workings of the British and American systems of government.

Basically, the three systems are the same in that they are solidly democratic. In each, representative government is based on universal suffrage. Although the names differ, political parties are the life-blood of the three systems and provide the means whereby each democracy can be organized to govern itself. British parties generally possess more clear-cut policies and appeal to definite sectors of the population, whereas American parties are similar to the Canadian ones in their attempts to appeal to a great variety of people in all walks of life and from one side of the continent to the other.

In each country, the government is based firmly on the rule of law as the surest safeguard against tyranny. All respect the rights of the individual, although the British have not built their guarantees into a written constitution, as the United States and Canada have done.

These are the fundamental aspects of the three governments. The exact methods used and the structure of government adopted in each case, however, differ sharply.

The Executive

Canada adopted a constitution that was expressly stated to be "similar in principle" to that of the United Kingdom. This meant that Canada was to be a parliamentary monarchy with the Queen represented by the Governor-General at the head, but with real executive authority vested in a Cabinet composed of ministers who were responsible to the legislature. Since the Crown acted only on the advice of ministers, and since the ministers were responsible to the legislature, which in turn was responsible, generally, to the people, there was one unbroken chain of authority in the government.

The United States, however, decided to be a republic with an elected President as the chief executive authority. Rather than see authority concentrated in a solid chain, the Americans preferred to see it divided. Afraid of excessive power in any one man or institution, they sought to create a *separation of powers* or a *system of checks and balances* in the constitution. Thus they separated the executive, the legislature and the judiciary and sought to make each one immune from encroachments by the other.

POWERS OF THE PRESIDENT

He is Commander-in-Chief of the Armed Forces.

He appoints diplomatic representatives and judges, subject to the approval of the Senate.

He keeps Congress informed of the state of the Union.

He may recommend measures to Congress.

He can veto bills passed by Congress; but the veto may be overridden by a two-thirds majority in both houses.

He can negotiate treaties with foreign countries; but they must be approved by the Senate.

He executes the laws of the United States.

He must preserve and defend the Constitution.

In theory, the President is not elected directly by the American people but by a body known as the Electoral College. Each state has a number of electors equal to the number of members it has in the House of Representatives and the Senate. The people in the states vote for their electors, who then vote for the President. In fact, however, the Electoral College is simply a long-outdated formality.

Each party nominates its candidate for President in a huge convention held the summer before the election. In each state, the party nominates members to stand for election to the Electoral College. These men are committed to vote for the party candidate and the people simply decide whether they want to support the Democratic or the Re-

THE GOVERNMENT OF THE UNITED STATES

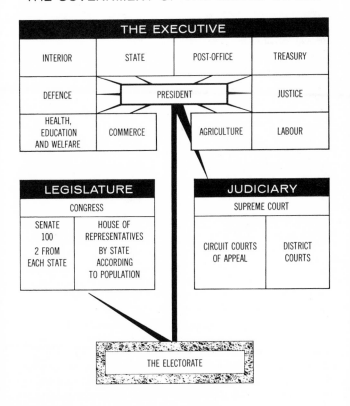

publican candidates for President and then vote for the electors who support the same party. Thus, in effect, the President is directly elected by the people at large.

The President holds office for four years regardless of what party controls the Congress, as the legislative branch is called. Congress is composed of two houses, the House of Representatives and the Senate. Since the House of Representatives is re-elected every two years and one-third of the Senate is re-elected every two years, with each senator then holding office for six years, it is often the case that a Republican President has to work with a Democratic Congress and vice versa. The President is not responsible for legislation; his duty is to keep Congress informed about "the state of the Union." He does this in his annual State of the Union message. He may also appear before Congress on other occasions to address the members and has the power to recommend measures for the consideration of Congress.

Congress may disregard the President's recommendations if it wishes. He in turn can veto any bill passed by Congress, although his veto can be overridden by a two-thirds vote in both houses. In Great Britain and Canada, the Prime Minister and his Cabinet sit in the legislature and direct its operation. In the United States neither the President nor his Cabinet can sit in the legislature. Cabinet members are responsible to the President alone. Thus in the United States there is no responsibility of the executive to the legislature, no single chain of authority, but a division of power and a system of checks and balances.

Many Americans have become highly critical of this aspect of their government and look with increasing favour upon our system of parliamentary or responsible government. They have seen Congress undermine a major defence programme by refusing to grant the President the money needed to put it in operation. They have seen Presidents reluctantly and half-heartedly sanction laws passed by Congress. In the diplomatic world, they have seen the President unable to make quick and absolute decisions because he must depend on the Senate to sanction any treaty. These weaknesses are apparent at any time, but when the President and Congress represent two hostile parties (as they did from 1956 to 1960, for example) and differ on major national policies, the activities of government may almost come to a full stop. They may also come to a stop during a presidential election when everyone knows (as did Mr. Khrushchev in 1960) that there will soon be a new President. Some attempts have been made to bring the executive and legislative branches closer together, but the division of power which was written into the Constitution almost two centuries ago still remains.

The Legislature

The second major distinction between the Canadian and British governments on the one hand and the American on the other lies in the legislative branch. All three countries have two legislative chambers. The House of Representatives in the United States, like the House of Commons in Canada and the United Kingdom, represents the people more or less on the basis of population. Unlike the House of Commons, however, the House of Representatives is by no means the supreme body. Sharing power with it and in many ways the dominant partner in Congress is the Senate.

Neither the British House of Lords nor the Canadian Senate has been able to maintain a powerful position in the legislature. The former is historically an aristocratic body, whose members owe their places to the accident of birth, and whose powers have been continually whittled away, the most famous occasion on which it suffered loss of authority being the passing of the Parliament Act of 1911. The Canadian Senate is an appointed body which on a few isolated occasions only has withstood the desires of the House of Commons. Neither the British House of Lords nor the Canadian Senate is based firmly on the popular will and thus must play a secondary role to that of the democratically elected House of Commons.

The American Senate, however, is elected. The Senator represents the people as much as the Representative in the lower house does. Moreover, as there are only two Senators for every state, each Senator represents more people than any member of the House of Representatives. Each one is elected for six years, whereas the member of the House of Representatives is elected for only two. Finally, the Senate is looked upon as the historic guardian of the rights of the states, a point to which we shall return.

For all these reasons, the upper house in Congress is in a far different position, and a stronger one, than its counterpart in Great Britain or Canada. Some Canadians have urged that their Senate be elected. The American experience might be useful in debating that question, for it has sometimes happened that the House of Representatives and the Senate have been controlled by opposing parties. This has an even more serious effect on the efficient working of government than does the split between the Congress as a whole and the President.

Unlike his Canadian counterpart the American Senator is a very important person in the public life of the country. He is an outstanding figure in his state, second only, if not superior, to the Governor (who is in state government what the President is in the national government). Often he is a candidate for the presidency. In the election of 1960 all candidates for President and Vice-President were, or had been, Senators. It is inconceivable that any Canadian Senator or any member of the House of Lords could ever be Prime Minister today. The American Senate is a much healthier institution in the democratic sense, but whether a country is better governed for having two elected branches of the legislature is a debatable point.

Federalism

Great Britain is a unitary state; this means that all power is possessed by one government, although some powers may be delegated to municipal and county authorities. Canada and the United States are federations in which power is shared by central and provincial (in Canada) or state (in the United States) governments. Thus, in the third feature of her governmental system, Canada is similar to the United States.

Just as the British North American colonies were to federate to solve their common problems and yet retain their individual identity in 1867, so the thirteen American colonies had federated in 1787 after their successful revolution against Britain. In the case of the American colonies, however, local feelings were stronger and the desire for a strong union less urgent than was the case in Canada. As a result, the American federal system was weaker at the centre or more decentralized than the Canadian system was to be almost a century later.

The American Senate has already given one piece of evidence to prove this point. The Senate was to be the guardian of states' rights in the national government. The two Senators from each state were originally chosen by the state legislature, although in 1913 this was changed to provide for direct election by the people in each state. Even so, the Senate still remains the bulwark of states' rights. Moreover, the Senate was given, and still possesses, some control over the President's power to appoint representatives abroad and to negotiate treaties.

The most important and conclusive feature of any federal system is the division of power between the central and state governments. In Canada the provinces were given specific powers of a local nature but the remaining or residual powers lay with the federal government. This was an obvious attempt to make the latter supreme. In the United States the authors of the Constitution gave the federal government specific powers, but the residual authority remained with the states. Under the circumstances of the time, the Canadians were determined that the central government should be strong; the Americans were determined to see that it was not too strong.

The development of American federalism has run in a different direction from that of Canada. The courts and political opinion were hostile to the extension of federal power in Canada, and as new functions of government became necessary, they fell within the provincial sphere. In the United States the courts have tended to be sympathetic to the expansion of federal activities. The so-called Elastic Clause, which gives the federal government all authority necessary to carry out its constitutional duty, and the Interstate Commerce Clause, have been used to justify and permit such an expansion. After the Civil War, northern political opinion also encouraged an expansion of federal authority for economic and nationalistic reasons. Thus, in relation to the many activities that modern governments undertake, the American administration has become more centralized while the Canadian federal system has become decentralized. Such is the irony of history.

POWERS OF CONGRESS

To levy taxes (The states too can levy taxes except for customs.)
To control foreign, inter-state and Indian trade
Defence and militia (The states may also have a militia.)
To make peace and war
Naturalization
To coin money, but not control banking
Post Office
To create courts (The states also have their own courts.)
To pass all laws necessary to carry out the powers given to it by the Constitution (This is the Elastic Clause, so called because it was expanded by the courts.)

In the field of foreign affairs, the original weakness of the central government and the doctrine of checks and balances can make matters very difficult. Since the Senate must ratify treaties and major appointments, the President can never be certain that his own wishes will be met. (Wilson, for example, saw the Senate refuse American membership in the League of Nations.) Nor can he guarantee that Congress will approve such matters as increased defence expenditures or foreign aid. If the President and the Congress are of two different parties, there may be a

THE TEN AMENDMENTS

1. Congress shall make no law respecting an establishment of religion, or prohibiting the free exercise thereof; or abridging the freedom of speech, or of the press; or the right of the people peaceably to assemble and to petition the government for a redress of grievances.

2. A well-regulated militia being necessary to the security of a free state, the right of the people to keep and bear arms shall not be infringed.

3. No soldier shall, in time of peace, be quartered in any house, without the consent of the owner, nor in time of war, but in a manner to be prescribed by law.

4. The right of the people to be secure in their persons, houses, papers, and effects, against unreasonable searches and seizures, shall not be violated; and no warrants shall issue but upon probable cause, supported by oath or affirmation, and particularly describing the place to be searched, and the persons or things to be seized.

5. No person shall be held to answer for a capital or otherwise infamous crime, unless on a presentment or indictment of a grand jury . . . ; nor shall any person be subject for the same offence to be twice put in jeopardy of life or limb, nor shall be compelled, in any criminal case, to be a witness against himself, nor be deprived of life, liberty or property, without due process of law; nor shall private property be taken for public use without just compensation.

6. In all criminal prosecutions, the accused shall enjoy the right to a speedy and public trial by an impartial jury . . . and to be informed of the nature and cause of the accusation; to be confronted with the witnesses against him; to have compulsory process for obtaining witnesses in his favor; and to have the assistance of counsel for his defence.

7. In suits at common law, where the value in controversy shall exceed twenty dollars, the right of trial by jury shall be preserved. . . .

8. Excessive bail shall not be required, nor excessive fines imposed, nor cruel and unusual punishments inflicted.

9. The enumeration in the Constitution of certain rights shall not be construed to deny or disparage others retained by the people.

10. The powers not delegated to the United States by the Constitution, nor prohibited by it to the states, are reserved to the states respectively, or to the people.

paralysis in policy and a lack of direction which in these critical days could be fatal.

Civil Liberties

Another distinguishing feature of the American Constitution is the existence of a Bill of Rights written into the Constitution at the time of its conception. The Americans felt that when their states were colonies of the British Empire they had suffered from arbitrary government. They were determined in their new Constitution to protect themselves against tyrannous action on the part of any government in the future. As a result, ten amendments were written into the Constitution almost as soon as it was adopted.

Following the Civil War, further amendments designed to assure the Negro equal political rights were passed. As with the other amendments, Congress was given power to enforce these rights, thus further extending its power. Without the post-Civil-War amendments, the federal government in the United States would not now have the power to force state governments to give equal rights to Negroes in education.

Although such fundamental rights as these are written down in the Constitution, there is no guarantee that they will be observed. Yet to those people sometimes denied such rights, it is comforting to know they exist in law and will be enforced by the courts. They also act as a constant reminder in the modern age that in a democratic country the rights of the individual are among the most sacred things on earth and cannot be destroyed or undermined by government. For that reason, as we have seen, many Canadians rejoice to see a Bill of Rights guaranteeing their civil liberties firmly embedded in Canadian law, written down for all men to see and observe.

These are only some of the outstanding differences in the form and operation of government in Canada, the United States and Great Britain. An entire year could be spent examining each one in detail. We hope that this introduction to the Canadian system of government has been sufficiently interesting to encourage you to read further on the subject.

A SHORT READING LIST

For detailed material the following volumes in the Canadian Government Series (University of Toronto Press) are useful.

J. A. Corry and J. E. Hodgetts, *Democratic Government and Politics*

R. MacG. Dawson, *The Government of Canada* (revised edition, edited by Norman Ward)

John Saywell, *The Office of Lieutenant-Governor*

Norman Ward, *The Canadian House of Commons*

Perhaps the most useful all-purpose reference work on government in Canada is *The Encyclopedia Canadiana* (Grolier).

Several pamphlets published by the Queen's Printer in Ottawa provide reasonable introductory surveys.

Canadian Citizenship Series No. 3, *Our System of Government*

E. R. Hopkins, *How Parliament Works*

W. J. Lawson, *The Canadian Constitution*

The Royal Canadian Mounted Police, *Law and Order in Canadian Democracy*

Other useful short studies of various aspects of Canadian government and politics are

R. MacG. Dawson, *Democratic Government in Canada* (University of Toronto Press)

J. H. S. Reid and others, *A Source-Book of Canadian History* (Longmans, Green)

F. H. Underhill, *Canadian Political Parties* (Canadian Historical Association Pamphlets)

Norman Ward, *Government in Canada* (Gage).

There are a number of new books on various aspects of Canadian government and politics that should be in every school library.

John Meisel, editor, *Papers on the 1962 Election* (University of Toronto Press). This volume contains an essay by Qualter and MacKirdy on the press of Ontario and the election.

John Porter, *The Vertical Mosaic* (University of Toronto Press)

Paul Fox, *Politics: Canada: Recent Readings*, third edition (McGraw-Hill)

J. Mallory, *The Structure of Canadian Government* (Macmillan)

Hugh G. Thorburn, *Party Politics in Canada* (Prentice-Hall)

D. Schmeiser, *Civil Liberties in Canada* (Oxford University Press)

Ramsay Cook, *Canada and the French-Canadian Question* (Macmillan)

John Saywell, *Quebec '70: A Documentary Narrative* (University of Toronto Press)

There are good studies of third parties, but none of either the Liberals or Conservatives. However, national party headquarters in Ottawa will usually send a packet of material on party platforms, which can provide a basis for analysis and discussion. Walter Young's *C.C.F.: The Anatomy of a Party* (University of Toronto Press) is an excellent account of a party facing the trade-offs between principles and power.

The *Canadian Annual Review* (John Saywell, editor) has been published by the University of Toronto Press since 1960 and provides an up-to-date survey of current developments in politics—provincial and national—, federal-provincial relations, and the growth of Quebec nationalism.

INDEX